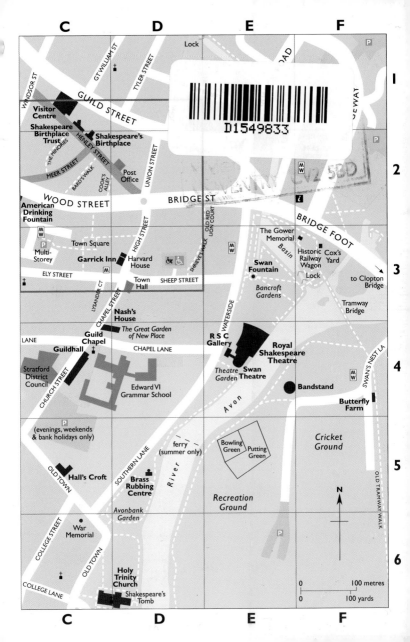

C   **D**   **E**   **F**

WINDSOR ST

GT WILLIAM ST

TYLER STREET

Lock

ROAD

WAY

1

GUILD STREET

D1549833

P

P

Visitor Centre

Shakespeare Birthplace Trust

HENLEY STREET

THE MINORIES

Shakespeare's Birthplace

MEER STREET

BARD'S WALK

COOK'S ALLEY

Union Street

Post Office

M W

CV2 5BD

2

WOOD STREET

BRIDGE ST

American Drinking Fountain

BRIDGE FOOT

M W

Town Square

HIGH STREET

SHRIEVE'S WALK

OLD RED LION COURT

M W

The Gower Memorial

Basin

Historic Railway Wagon

Cox's Yard

3

P

Multi-Storey

Garrick Inn

Harvard House

♿ ♿

Swan Fountain

Lock

to Clopton Bridge

ELY STREET

M

SHEEP STREET

Town Hall

Bancroft Gardens

Tramway Bridge

LYSANDER CT

CHAPEL STREET

Nash's House

The Great Garden of New Place

WATERSIDE

R S C Gallery

SWAN'S NEST LA

4

LANE

Guild Chapel

CHAPEL LANE

Royal Shakespeare Theatre

Guildhall

CHURCH STREET

Stratford District Council

Edward VI Grammar School

Theatre Garden

Swan Theatre

Bandstand

M W

Butterfly Farm

Avon

P

(evenings, weekends & bank holidays only)

SOUTHERN LANE

ferry (summer only)

Bowling Green

Putting Green

Cricket Ground

OLD TRAMWAY WALK

5

OLD TOWN

Hall's Croft

Brass Rubbing Centre

River

COLLEGE STREET

Avonbank Garden

War Memorial

Recreation Ground

N

OLD TOWN

6

COLLEGE LANE

Holy Trinity Church

Shakespeare's Tomb

0   100 metres

0   100 yards

C   **D**   **E**   **F**

JARROLD
publishing

STRATFORD

...MORE THAN A GUIDE

ANNIE BULLEN

CITY-BREAK GUIDES

Acknowledgements

Photography © Jarrold Publishing by Neil Jinkerson.
Additional photography by kind permission of:
Shakespeare Birthplace Trust; Brass Rubbing Centre.

The publishers wish to thank Sue Croxford (Shakespeare Birthplace Trust) and Veronica Tanner (TIC) for their invaluable assistance; also the many owners of Stratford businesses for their kindness in allowing us to photograph their premises.

Printed in Singapore.
ISBN 0 7117 2647 7   1/04

Designer: Simon Borrough
Editor: Angela Royston
Artwork and walk maps: Clive Goodyer
City maps: The Map Studio, Romsey, Hants. Main map based on cartography © George Philip Ltd

Front cover:
Jester statue in Henley Street

Previous page:
Shakespeare's Birthplace garden

CONTENTS

Stratford-upon-Avon, tucked into a pretty pocket of English countryside and displaying picturesque evidence of its 800-year history in every street, would be a lure to visitors, even without its connection with William Shakespeare. But the small Warwickshire town, on the banks of the wide River Avon, can't escape its legacy. The world's greatest playwright was born and died here. Buildings and streets that would have been familiar to him still exist, some

WELCOME TO STRATFORD

largely unchanged. An internationally regarded theatre complex flourishes, while houses belonging to Shakespeare and his family can be explored.

As in Tudor days, the town's tranquil riverside areas give a feeling of peace and space, but time doesn't stand still in Stratford. Visitors come to explore Shakespeare's life, but they also enjoy the vibrancy of the present – the stylish shops and restaurants, and the unique feel of a town set apart by its history.

River Avon

HIGHLIGHTS

Shakespeare the man and Shakespeare the writer are what many people come to Stratford to discover. But once you've visited his family homes and seen his works performed at the theatre, you'll find that Stratford has plenty in reserve. Here are some of the essentials to help you get a feel of this historic town. (Note that most places are closed from 23–26 December.)

Shakespeare's Birthplace

SHAKESPEARE'S BIRTH-PLACE AND EXHIBITION
Henley Street; map C1–C2

This is at the heart of the Shakespeare story; an award-winning exhibition, giving you a picture of the writer's life from cradle to grave. When you've seen the exhibition, cross the garden to visit the house where William, his parents and his five brothers and sisters lived. There are five 'Shakespeare houses' in Stratford but this one is the most intimately connected with the man, and you will go away with some idea of the influences that inspired his work. Historians have done a marvellous job from the comparatively little documentary evidence that exists concerning Shakespeare, but you will probably wish we knew more. Look for Shakespeare's will in the Shakespeare Exhibition and figure out why he chose to leave the bulk of his property to his elder daughter, Susanna.

Open: daily; opening times vary – ring to check
Entry: under £10
Tel: 01789 201832
Further information: pages 48–49

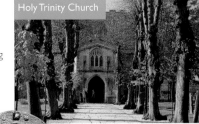
Holy Trinity Church

Sanctuary knocker

HOLY TRINITY CHURCH
Old Town; map C6/D6

This is reckoned to be the most visited parish church in England. Everyone wants to see Shakespeare's grave, but most go away captivated by the sheer beauty of the well-kept church on the banks of the Avon.

Look for the 'weeping chancel' – this is where the poet is buried; the chancel itself is built at a slight angle, said to represent the slant of Christ's head on the Cross. Look too for the lively carving on the misericords, or 'ledges', on the choir stalls and the 1611 Bible on display in the chancel.

Open: daily; Mar–Oct: Mon–Sat 8.30–18.00, Sun 14.00–17.00; Nov–Feb: Mon–Sat 9.00–16.00, Sun 14.00–17.00. The church may be closed if there are special services or concerts
Entry: free, but you are asked for £1 (50p for students and concessions) to see Shakespeare's tomb and there is a church donations box
Further information: pages 40–41

Shakespeare Exhibition

Royal Shakespeare Theatre

ROYAL SHAKESPEARE THEATRE
Waterside; map E4

You can't miss this solid red-brick building dominating the town bank of the River Avon. This is where you'll see world class performances of Shakespeare's works. The other theatre in the complex, the distinctive Swan, has a comprehensive programme of performance too. You can take a backstage tour and eat in the restaurant or café-bar, which has the unusual name of 1564.

Open: ring box office for performance times; the café-bar daily from 10.30 for coffee and light meals
Tel: box office 01789 403403; backstage tours 01789 403405; information/booking line 0870 6091110
Further information: pages 46–47

NASH'S HOUSE AND NEW PLACE
Chapel Street; map C4

New Place, one of the most substantial houses in Stratford, was bought by

M O N E Y   S A V E R S
You can buy a ticket which admits you to the three Shakespeare properties in Stratford – Shakespeare's Birthplace, Hall's Croft and Nash's House – for under £10. A ticket that also includes the two out-of-town properties – Anne Hathaway's Cottage and Mary Arden's House – is under £15. Both tickets are valid for one year from the date that you buy the ticket.

Shakespeare in 1597 as his family home. Unfortunately it was demolished just over 150 years later. You can see the foundations, and an Elizabethan knot garden. Entry is through the next-door property, Nash's House, once owned by Thomas Nash who married Elizabeth, Shakespeare's granddaughter. Here you'll see a museum devoted to Stratford before and after Shakespeare's time. Behind both properties is The Great Garden, reached through a gateway in Chapel Lane and the setting for some inspiring sculpture.

Nash's House

Open: daily; opening times vary – ring to check
Entry: Nash's House under £5; New Place free
Tel: 01789 292325
Further information: pages 43–44

ANNE HATHAWAY'S COTTAGE
Shottery
One of the most photographed houses anywhere in the world. You'll experience a jolt of recognition as you approach the cottage, once occupied by Shakespeare's wife. The interior is much as it would have been in the 16th century except for the 'museum room', which displays a collection of items associated with the house over the centuries.

Getting there: B439 towards Evesham and follow the signs to Shottery and the cottage
Open: daily; opening times vary – ring to check
Entry: around £5
Tel: 01789 292100
Further information: pages 33–34

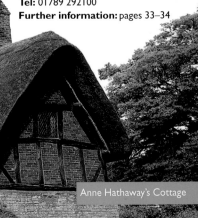
Anne Hathaway's Cottage

A WALK ALONG WATERSIDE

Starting at the Gower Memorial of Shakespeare in Bancroft Gardens (map F3), walk along Waterside, past the theatres and the Brass Rubbing Centre (page 34) to Holy Trinity Church (page 40). Call in on the way at The Dirty Duck (properly, but almost never, called The Black Swan) (map D4) for a drink, a bite to eat and a bit of star-spotting. This is the pub where the actors from the RST (Royal Shakespeare Theatre) hang out.

The Gower Memorial

UGLY DUCKLING?

You might do a double-take as you walk past the popular Black Swan pub on Waterside. The sign shows an elegant swan on one side – and a cartoon-style duck on the other, acknowledging that the pub is always referred to as 'The Dirty Duck'.

BUTTER-FLY FARM

Tramway Walk, Swan's Nest Lane; map F4

A lush and lovely rainforest filled with pools, waterfalls and hundreds of exotic butterflies is to be found in Europe's largest butterfly farm. There are other creepy-crawlies here too. Look for the world's largest spider in the terrifying-sounding Arachnoland – happily in a sealed compartment.

Open: daily; summer: 10.00–18.00; winter: 10.00–dusk
Entry: under £5
Further information: pages 34–35

A DRINK IN STRATFORD'S OLDEST PUBS

The Garrick in the High Street and the unpretentious and very old Windmill in Church Street are two pubs not to be missed (see pages 74–75 for more).

Guild Chapel

HALL'S CROFT
Old Town; map C5
Shakespeare's elder daughter, Susanna, and her husband, eminent physician Dr John Hall, lived here after their marriage in 1607. You'll find a large and well-furnished house, which includes a doctor's consulting-room of the time and a garden growing many of the medicinal plants which the apothecaries would have used.

Open: daily; opening times vary – ring to check
Entry: under £5
Tel: 01789 292107
Further information: page 38

Hall's Croft

GUILD CHAPEL
Chapel Street; map C4
The Guild of the Holy Cross, to which most of Stratford's influential merchants and businessmen belonged, built a chapel here in 1269. The Reformation saw the obliteration of the wall paintings with which it was decorated. Now some have been uncovered and may be viewed. Look for a Day of Judgement painting (known as 'Doom') over the chancel arch, and St Thomas Becket and St George on the west wall.

Open: daily; Thu–Tue 9.45–16.15, Wed 11.00–16.15. (May be closed occasionally for special services)
Entry: free – there's a donations box inside
Further information: page 37

HARVARD HOUSE AND THE MUSEUM OF BRITISH PEWTER
High Street; map D3
This, the most ornately decorated house in Stratford, contains an internationally important pewter collection. The house belonged to the mother of John Harvard, who founded the American university named after him. It is now owned by the university but is managed by the Shakespeare Birthplace Trust.

Open: Easter–end Oct; days and times vary – ring to check
Entry: under £5
Tel: 01789 204016 or 01789 204507
Further information: page 39

Harvard House

TREAT YOURSELF
Visit Martini's Delicatessen in The Minories (map C2). You can buy excellent food here for a picnic by the river, or to take home.

BRASS RUBBING CENTRE
The RST Summer House, Avonbank Garden; map D5
There's a huge collection of medieval and Tudor brasses here, giving lots of clues to the past. You can look at the unique collection, buy ready-rubbed 'pictures', or do it yourself from as little as £1. They'll show you what to do and provide the materials.
Open: summer: daily 10.00–18.00; winter: 11.00–16.00 on some days (ring to check whether open)
Entry: free to view exhibition
Tel: 01789 297671
Further information: page 34

Mary Arden's House

MARY ARDEN'S HOUSE
Wilmcote, 3 miles on A3400

For many years, there was confusion over which of the farmhouses in Wilmcote, just outside Stratford, was the family home of Mary Arden, Shakespeare's mother. Now we know she was brought up at Glebe Farm, known as Mary Arden's House. You'll also see an interesting and lively farm museum at nearby Palmer's Farm.

Open: daily; opening times vary – ring to check
Entry: around £5
Tel: 01789 293455
Further information: page 42

Portrait of Shakespeare by Gerald Soest

DISCOVERING SHAKESPEARE

Every day we use words and phrases introduced into the English language by William Shakespeare. How did a boy, born to a glove maker in a small Midlands town and educated to the age of 14 at the local grammar school, develop the ability to turn the English language into a tool so potent that his works have the power to move and delight nearly 500 years after they were written?

Shakespeare's influence on English language, literature and culture is greater than that of any other single writer; experts tell us he had an immense vocabulary of 30,000 words – at least 2,000 of these coined by him and still used today. We can only guess at the influences in his home town that nurtured this talent: a classical education, daily listening to the resounding words and phrases of the Bible, close observation of men and

PUSH-BUTTON WILL
Shakespeare's last will and testament is a complicated document, which is hard to decipher. But the Shakespeare Exhibition in Henley Street makes it easy to work out who got what by providing a large push-button chart.

Shakespeare's will

women going about their business in a prosperous market town. The river and the wooded countryside around Stratford must have played their part too in firing his imagination.

We know that Shakespeare was born in Stratford on or around 23 April 1564. He died at his home in the town exactly 52 years later. We know who his parents were and where he spent his childhood. He married Anne Hathaway, eight years his senior and pregnant with their first child, when he was just 18. He was only 20 when their twins, Judith and Hamnet, were born. But nothing is known for certain about how or why his career in the theatre came about.

HAMNET AND JUDITH

Shakespeare's twins, Hamnet and Judith, were named after his friends, Stratford baker Hamnet Sadler and his wife, Judith. Sadly young Hamnet died in 1596, aged 11. His father, writing *King John*, has Constance, whose son has disappeared, poignantly say:
'Grief fills the room up of my absent child,
Lies in his bed, walks up and down with me,
Puts on his pretty looks, repeats his words,
Remembers me of all his gracious parts,
Stuffs out his vacant garments with his form.'

Schoolroom in the Guildhall

He arrived in London and, by the age of 27, had tasted success as an actor and writer, with several plays performed and acclaimed. By 30 he was a leading member of the foremost company of actors, the Lord Chamberlain's Men (later known as the King's Men) and a substantial shareholder in the newly built Globe Theatre. Ten years later, a man of substance, he was part of the royal household. He was canny with money, investing in property in his home town, where he retired in comfort in 1613.

You can flesh out these bare facts by visiting the Shakespeare houses and Shakespeare Exhibition, by walking the streets he would have known and allowing your imagination to build its own picture of the world's greatest playwright.

Shakespeare Centre and Birthplace Exhibition

THE CLOPTON CONNECTION

If William Shakespeare had not been born, Stratford's most written-about son would probably have been Hugh Clopton, who was born in the town in the 15th century. Like Dick Whittington, the young Hugh left his native town to make his fortune. He succeeded, becoming a successful mercer, buying and selling fine cloth. Like Dick Whittington, Hugh was also offered, and accepted, one of the top jobs in London – that of Lord Mayor. He was to hold the post for one year, in 1491.

UNDERNEATH THE ARCHES Hugh Clopton's gift to Stratford-upon-Avon of a finely constructed bridge has served the town well for more than 500 years. But the bridge lives on in more ways than one – Clopton Bridge is the name given to an energetic barn dance which is devised for sets of four couples.

Clopton Bridge

Hugh Clopton never married, nor did he forget his native town. When he left for the bustle of the capital, he would have crossed the River Avon by way of the existing rickety and hazardous wooden bridge. His major gift to Stratford was the construction of the fine, 14-arched stone bridge that spans the river today, bearing the weight of constant traffic. The Clopton bridge took ten years to build from 1480.

Other evidence of his generosity can still be seen in the Guild Chapel which he enlarged and improved with the addition of the tower. You can see a stained-glass window depicting this benefactor in the Chapel. Hugh also initiated welfare schemes for local boys and girls and paid for improvements to the roads – which did much to help encourage and sustain Stratford's trade.

There's a memorial chapel to him and to the Clopton family in Holy Trinity Church, although he did not occupy the tomb prepared for him there but was buried instead in London. The fine tombs of later members of the Clopton family can be admired, especially that of George Carew, Earl of Totnes, and Baron Clopton (1555–1629) and his wife, Joyce. George became Master in Ordnance to King James I and you'll notice the cannon, cannon balls and muskets carved on the tomb.

There is a link between Hugh Clopton and Stratford's other notable citizen. Hugh built himself a fine house of brick and timber, standing in pretty gardens no more than a stone's throw from the Guild Chapel. Over 100 years later, in 1597, the same house, New Place, was bought by William Shakespeare to be his own family home.

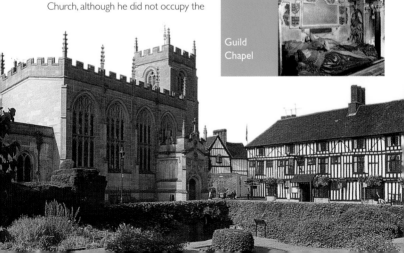

George Carew's tomb

Guild Chapel

PLANNING YOUR VISIT

A day is not enough to see everything that Stratford has to offer, but, if that's all you have, here are some suggestions to help you make the most of your visit. And if you do have longer to spend here, you'll find plenty of ideas to fill two or three days very pleasantly.

> **MARRY IN HASTE...**
> When young Will did the decent thing and married Anne Hathaway in 1582, the banns were read in church not three times, as was customary, but only once. This was because Anne was pregnant and the marriage was by special licence.

THE FIRST DAY

How did the son of a tradesman in a little market town learn to use words that have translated effortlessly across countries and centuries? You won't find all the answers at the Shakespeare Birthplace and Exhibition in Henley Street (see page 48) because there's a lot we don't know about Shakespeare, but you'll be fascinated by what you learn about the poet himself and life in the town at the time.

If you're keen to see more, it's worth buying a combined ticket to all three Shakespeare Houses in the town (it's valid for up to one year). Before you set off to see Nash's House and New Place (viewed together) and Hall's Croft, take a break to enjoy coffee and a pastry at Drucker's near the Birthplace, or at Havilands in nearby Meer Street.

Shakespeare would have seen the Guild Chapel (see page 37) every day of his life in Stratford. When younger he would have sat inside it for a daily service with his fellow pupils from the grammar school next door. In later years he bought a house across the way. Pop in to see the restored wall paintings and enjoy the peaceful atmosphere. Take a look down Church Street (map C4) for a perfect picture of well-preserved half-timbered buildings.

Drucker's, Henley Street

Church Street

Now you can enjoy the riverside, busy with boats and alive with the swans for which the town is famous. If you feel thirsty, the café-bar in the Royal Shakespeare Theatre (map E4), with its sunny terrace opening onto the river-bank, is a good place for a cup of tea and a quiet contemplation of the Avon. Turn back into the town centre via Sheep Street (map D3–E3) for a browse round the shops, many of them independently owned.

Take time for a leisurely lunch at one of Stratford's excellent pubs or restaurants (see pages 65–76) before a stroll towards the river, via Holy Trinity Church (see page 40) where Shakespeare and members of his family are buried.

THE NEXT TWO OR THREE DAYS

You will by now have seen the three Shakespeare town houses and had a flavour of the geography of Stratford with its wide river and medieval streets, laid out in a fairly uniform grid pattern.

Holy Trinity Church

Royal Shakespeare Theatre

Old Bank, Chapel Street

If you have longer than one day to spend here, what you do now depends largely on your own tastes – you should find plenty to satisfy them. Here are some 'pick and mix' suggestions to help you enjoy Stratford.

Shakespeare in the country
If you enjoyed the town houses and can't get enough of the 'Sweet Swan of Avon', pay a visit to the two country properties that would have been well known to the young Shakespeare. If the weather's fine you can walk to Anne Hathaway's Cottage (see page 28), just over a kilometre (less than a mile) from the town centre. Young William presumably trod

> **ABOUT SWANNING**
> Swans have always been a feature of Stratford life. The jolly ceremony of 'swan-hopping' (a corruption of the more usual 'swan-upping') was held annually in the late 19th century when ladies and gentlemen would row from Lucy's Mill to corral the birds and mark them. Once that was done they could enjoy themselves with a picnic or perhaps alcoholic refreshment.

this path many times when he was courting Anne. We do know that when they married in 1582, Anne was already expecting their first daughter, Susanna. Mary Arden was Shakespeare's mother and her home was a farm about 5 kilometres (3 miles) from town. When you visit this house you can also see the nearby Countryside Museum, so allow plenty of time to visit both.

Tour bus

Open-top tours

Put yourself in the hands of the expert guides on the colourful open-top buses that leave the Pen and Parchment by the Tourist Information Centre (map F2) and Cox's Yard (by Tramway Bridge) at regular intervals (see page 82). They visit the Shakespeare houses and other places of interest. A ticket lasts for 24 hours and you may hop on and off as often as you like.

All the world's a stage

In Stratford quite a lot of it is. Check out the programmes for a matinee or an evening performance at the Royal Shakespeare Theatre (see page 46) and the Swan. If you'd like to know more about the working of one of the world's greatest theatres, book a backstage tour. Details on page 83.

Shopping spree

Take time to explore the charming old streets, courtyards and alleyways of Stratford and you might be surprised at the range of goodies on offer. If you're searching for something old and interesting, the Ely Street Antiques Market (map C3) is a good place to start, with more than 50 units selling a variety of different antiques. Stratford is blessed with good coffee shops, so you needn't go hungry or thirsty during your quest.

Stratford on foot

While you're exploring on foot, why not follow one of our walks (see pages

Ely Street antiques

Sheep Street

their haunts. You can join the weekly evening ghost walk (see page 79) or visit The Falstaff Experience in Sheep Street (see page 36) where they will scare the pants off you.

Stratford alfresco

Buy sandwiches or put together a picnic from Martini's Deli in the Minories, Munchies in Meer Street, Chadds in Union Street or one of the barges in the Canal Basin (map E3) and enjoy it on the banks of the Avon in Bancroft Gardens or the Recreation Ground, or in the more peaceful Great Garden off Chapel Lane (map D4). You can hire bicycles (see page 95) or, if you prefer, a canoe, punt or rowing boat (see page 82) and enjoy a lazy hour or so on the water.

The baguette barge

Tropical paradise

Huge, brightly coloured, exotic butter-flies, fluttering in a man-made rainforest complete with waterfalls and pools, are what you will find at the Butterfly Farm (see page 34). It is said to be the largest of its kind in Europe and there's certainly plenty to see.

Enjoy the food

There are some excellent restaurants and pubs of all sorts in the town. Look through pages 65–76 and take your pick. It's a good idea to book at busy times.

26–31) which will not only show you some of the town's history but also give you a feel for the Stratford-upon-Avon of today? The walks will take you past some of its taverns. Whether you choose to explore them further is up to you.

Scary Stratford

A town as old as this is bound to be crawling with ghosts – and there are people only too happy to show you

WALKS

There's history and interest with every step you take in the medieval town of Stratford. We've devised three walks, which each lasts about 90 minutes, or longer if you stop at places on the way. The first walk is dedicated to Shakespeare, the second is a short cross-country stroll to his wife's girlhood home, and the third walk explores the history of the town with plenty of opportunities for shopping.

SHAKESPEARE'S TOWN WALK

If Shakespeare could revisit the town of his birth, would he recognize the buildings and the layout of modern-day Stratford streets? This walk starts at the Birthplace, Shakespeare's boyhood home in Henley Street. He'd recognize the house, although the entrance is altered, but he'd be astounded at the lack of dirt and everyday smells of Elizabethan England. He might be upset to learn that the houses next door had been demolished to lessen fire risk.

Walk down Henley Street towards the bridge, turning right into Meer Street. You'll reach Rother Market, where John Shakespeare, William's father, bought the animal hides that he turned into fine gloves. Again it might all seem a bit clinical to William, who would remember bloody hides and carcasses. Carry on down Rother Street and then creep, snail-like, with

him along Scholars Lane to the left, to revisit his old school. School was an upper room in the Guildhall (see page 38), largely unchanged. Next door is the Guild Chapel (see page 37). He would be surprised to see the restored wall paintings, covered over in his time by Reformist zealots.

A tear might well up when he spied the great gap across the lane where his fine house, New Place (see page 43), once stood. Walk down Chapel Lane into his Great Garden and marvel at the sculptures there, representing his works. Turn back into Church Street, following the road round to the left,

The Great Garden

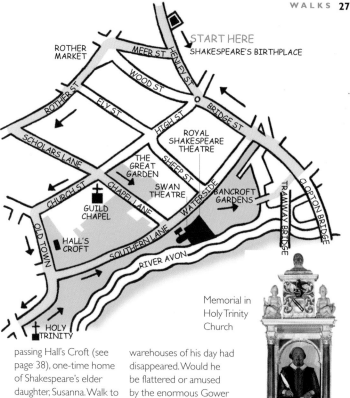

START HERE
SHAKESPEARE'S BIRTHPLACE

ROTHER MARKET

MEER ST

HENLEY ST

WOOD ST

BRIDGE ST

ROTHER ST

FLY ST

SCHOLARS LANE

HIGH ST

ROYAL SHAKESPEARE THEATRE

THE GREAT GARDEN

SHEEP ST

CHURCH ST

CHAPEL LANE

SWAN THEATRE

WATERSIDE

BANCROFT GARDENS

GUILD CHAPEL

TRAMWAY BRIDGE

CLOPTON BRIDGE

OLD TOWN

HALL'S CROFT

SOUTHERN LANE

RIVER AVON

HOLY TRINITY

Memorial in Holy Trinity Church

passing Hall's Croft (see page 38), one-time home of Shakespeare's elder daughter, Susanna. Walk to Holy Trinity Church (see page 40) in Old Town. Shakespeare was a lay rector, which is why his tomb has its prominent place in the chancel.

Go back along Waterside, past the theatres dedicated to his work and into Bancroft Gardens. He'd spy the familiar Clopton Bridge but would wonder why the wharves and

warehouses of his day had disappeared. Would he be flattered or amused by the enormous Gower Memorial, a sculpture showing him surrounded by four of his most well-known characters?

Walk up Bridge Street past old Market Place, where his father sold leather goods. Less happy memories would be evoked by the shop on the corner of the High Street. It's where his younger daughter Judith

lived with her ne'er-do-well husband, Thomas Quiney, a man disliked by Shakespeare. Return by Henley Street to the Birthplace, with the knowledge that some things change little over the centuries.

Tavern Lane, Shottery

THE PRIMROSE PATH OF DALLIANCE WALK

This is a walk of about 5 kilometres (3 miles), best made on a fine day. It takes you from the town centre out to Anne Hathaway's Cottage (see page 33), returning by a different route. Allow about an hour and a quarter for the walk, plus time for visiting the cottage – and the pub. We must assume that Shakespeare himself often trod these paths while out courting Anne Hathaway, his future wife.

A good starting point is The Swan Fountain in Bancroft Gardens, near the Royal Shakespeare Theatre. Turn your back on the river, crossing Waterside to reach the bottom of Sheep Street. Walk up Sheep Street and over the crossroads into Ely Street, turning left at the end into Rother Street. Cross the road towards The Firs Garden

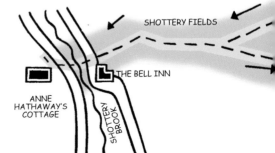

SHOTTERY FIELDS

THE BELL INN

ANNE HATHAWAY'S COTTAGE

SHOTTERY BROOK

at the end of Rother Street. Walk through the gardens into Grove Road and cross into Albany Road which bears round to the right. As you clear the corner, start looking for the footpath sign on the left pointing to Anne Hathaway's Cottage.

Brook Walk, Shottery

Follow this paved footpath into Shottery Fields, passing a children's playground and bearing right. You'll see signs to the cottage via Tavern Lane. Go past some lovely old cottages and a horticultural centre to reach the Bell Inn at Shottery. You may be tempted inside to quench your thirst; once you are refreshed, either carry on down Cottage Lane ahead or, if the gate is not locked, down Jubilee Path which

leads over Shottery Brook. Both paths will take you to the cottage.

When it's time to return, retrace your steps to the Bell Inn, then go past the thatched cottages on the left towards Shottery Fields. At the field, bear right, following the footpath signposted towards Hall's Croft (see page 38). This will bring you back

into Stratford at Evesham Place; carry on down Chestnut Walk to Hall's Croft, the one-time home of Shakespeare's daughter Susanna and her husband, Dr John Hall, an eminent physician. At the end of the road, turn left into Southern Lane, strolling back through Avonbank Garden, past the theatres, to the Swan Fountain.

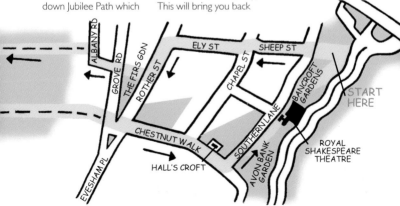

SHOPPER'S WALK

This walk is really a gentle stroll around the town's streets, giving you plenty of opportunity to explore the many little courts and shopping alleys while still seeing some of Stratford's historic buildings.

Start at the top of Henley Street so that you can admire the joyful statue of the jester, given to the town by Tony Bird. Walk down towards the town, passing the Shakespeare

Exhibition and the Birthplace (see page 48) before turning right along Meer Street. This opens out into Rother Market. Cross the end of Windsor Street to take a look at

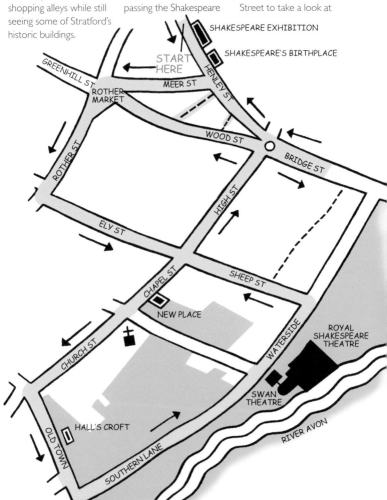

SHAKESPEARE EXHIBITION

SHAKESPEARE'S BIRTHPLACE

START HERE

GREENHILL ST

HENLEY ST

MEER ST

ROTHER MARKET

ROTHER ST

WOOD ST

BRIDGE ST

HIGH ST

ELY ST

SHEEP ST

CHAPEL ST

NEW PLACE

CHURCH ST

WATERSIDE

ROYAL SHAKESPEARE THEATRE

SWAN THEATRE

HALL'S CROFT

OLD TOWN

SOUTHERN LANE

RIVER AVON

The Teddy Bear Museum

left (good fashion shops and restaurants). At the end turn right into the High Street, go past The Garrick Inn and make your way to the end where the market cross once stood on what is now the mini roundabout. On your right is Crabtree and Evelyn. This old building used to be a gaol and, later, the home of Shakespeare's younger daughter Judith. Now you can turn left into Wood Street or right into Bridge Street. Then turn back up Henley Street, exploring Cook's Alley and Bard's Walk on the way.

The Garrick Inn

The Teddy Bear Museum (see page 50) in Greenhill Street. Cross back into Rother Street and carry on until you spot Ely Street on your left. If you like browsing around antique shops you might go no further once you spot the renowned Antiques Market here.

If you do make it to Chapel Street look at the carvings on the HSBC Bank on the corner. You'll also find some nice old pubs in this part of town. Along the way, as Chapel Street becomes Church Street, you'll pass the site of Shakespeare's house – the now demolished New Place, the Guild Chapel, the old Guildhall (see page 38) and the almshouses. Follow the curve of the road into Old Town, past Hall's Croft (see page 38) and then turn left into Southern Lane.

Continue until you turn into Sheep Street on the

The American Fountain

You could be forgiven for thinking that Stratford is simply a shrine dedicated to the memory of William Shakespeare. Of course this is the place to find out everything that is known about Britain's great playwright (and you might be surprised to discover how many gaps there are in our knowledge about his life), but there's a lot more to Stratford than Shakespeare. Had he not existed, the pretty little town with its half-timbered buildings and riverside walks would still be a magnet attracting visitors; the places to visit reflect the charm of the town as much as the legacy of the poet. If you are visiting around Christmas, remember that most places are shut from 23–26 December.

S I G H T S E E I N G

The American Fountain
Rother Market; map B2
This large Gothic clock tower used to have a built-in fountain, but the water troughs are now generally planted with flowers. It was presented to the town by George W. Childs of Philadelphia to mark Queen Victoria's Golden Jubilee in 1897. Actor Henry Irving carried out the unveiling. If you look closely, you will see not only American eagles but also English lions and, watching over each of the clock faces, a fairy from *A Midsummer Night's Dream*.

Anne Hathaway's Cottage
Shottery
Can there be a household in the land that has not at one time had a tea towel, calendar, jigsaw puzzle or postcard that shows the exterior of the one-time home of Shakespeare's wife, Anne Hathaway? If you look at the long, low house from the garden, you'll see it appears to be built in two sections. The oldest part of the building, and the one that Shakespeare would have known when he was courting Anne, is that on the right. The higher, left-hand part of the house was probably not built until 1623, seven years after his death in 1616.

Anne Hathaway's Cottage

The cottage is as charming as it appears on all those pictures, although you must remember that the well-tended garden would have been a farmyard when the Bard was alive. The interior looks much as it would have done in Shakespeare's day, apart from the collection of items associated with the house over the centuries which is displayed in the 'museum room'. Outside, in addition to the cottage garden, there is a maturing tree garden, maze and sculpture collection. If you are staying in Stratford and want to stretch your legs, the cottage is about a one-kilometre (less than a mile) walk and is well signposted from the town centre.

Getting there: B439 towards Evesham and follow the signs to Shottery and the cottage

Open: daily; opening times vary – ring to check

Entry: around £5. You can buy tickets which admit you to some or all of the Shakespeare properties – see page 8 for details

Tel: 01789 292100

Website: www.shakespeare.org.uk

Disabled access: none to house

Other facilities: tea garden (open Mar–Oct)

Brass Rubbing Centre

The RST Summer House, Avonbank Garden; map D5

The medieval and Tudor brasses here tell a fascinating story of the social life and times of their periods. Very often brass plates were placed in churches in memory of the dead, so they paint an accurate picture of the past, allowing a glimpse of social customs, trades and dress. You can look at the unique collection, buy ready-rubbed 'pictures', or have a go yourself. Rubbing charges vary from 95p for a small brass to £19.95 for a large portrait. Help and advice are given and there are special 'rubbing rates' and a demonstration for pre-booked groups of ten or more.

Open: summer: daily 10.00–18.00; winter: 11.00–16.00 on some days (ring to check whether open)

Entry: free, although there are charges for brass rubbing (see above)

Tel: 01789 297671

Website: www.stratford. co.uk/brass

Disabled access: full

Other facilities: gift shop

Brass Rubbing Centre

Butterfly Farm

Tramway Walk, Swan's Nest Lane; map F4

You might not fancy getting up close and personal to the world's largest spider, but kids will love it. In fact the deadly creatures of Arachnoland are housed safely in sealed glass compartments at the Butterfly Farm, which is just five minutes' walk from Stratford's town centre. It is Europe's largest such attraction and very pleasant too, with a lush, warm 'rainforest' alive with hundreds of exotic butterflies, beautiful flowering

Clopton Bridge

plants and fish-filled pools. The whole life cycle of the butterflies is explained in the Caterpillar Room. Insect City has fascinating inhabitants, including stick insects, leaf-cutting ants and beetles, all of which can be closely examined.

Open: daily; summer: 10.00–18.00; winter: 10.00–dusk
Entry: under £5
Tel: 01789 299288
Website: www.butterflyfarm.co.uk
Disabled access: full
Other facilities: gift shop, children's adventure playground and wildlife garden/butterfly meadow

Clopton Bridge
off map F3

If you come into the town from the south, you'll probably drive over this wonderful old stone bridge, which was built in the 15th century but still copes perfectly well with the weight of heavy traffic in the 21st century. It has 14 arches spanning the River Avon. The bridge, like later parts of the Guild Chapel (see page 37), was paid for by Hugh Clopton, Lord Mayor of London in 1491 and man of property and benefactor in London and Stratford.

STRATFORD IN SHAKESPEARE'S TIME
When Shakespeare was born, Stratford – a vital river crossing – was one of the most important market towns in Warwickshire. It wasn't large, with only around 2,000 inhabitants. The well-spaced streets and houses were interspersed with orchards, gardens and large clusters of trees. Business was varied, with four markets selling corn, malt, crafts, dairy produce, meat, cattle, horses and sheep. John Shakespeare, William's father, was one of several glove makers in Stratford, who set up his stall at the market cross where Henley Street and the High Street converge.

FLUTTERING BY
The Butterfly Farm is home to the world's most brightly-coloured butterfly – you can't fail to enjoy the many, large, intensely coloured South American Blue Morphos fluttering free in the butterfly area.

Country Artists Visitor Centre
The Mill, Avenue Farm
Here you'll find thousands of animals and country subjects, made and hand-painted on site from original sculptures. Bird sculptures in particular are a speciality and are pounced on by collectors. Guides will take you through the whole process, although the main part of the tour concentrates on the painting studios, where artists bring the sculptures to life with the (extremely skilled) flick of a brush. New items are added to the range in January and July each year.
Getting there: from the town centre take the A3400 towards Birmingham. In less than a mile you'll see Avenue Farm on your left
Open: daily; Mon–Sat 9.00–17.00; Sun 10.00–16.00; studio tours Mon–Fri only (best to book)
Entry: free, including studio tours
Tel: 01789 200722
Website: www.countryartists.co.uk
Disabled access: full
Other facilities: factory shop

The Falstaff Experience
Sheep Street; map D3
The reputedly much-haunted Shrieves House in Sheep Street is the setting for the theatrical Falstaff Experience. You enter through enormous old wooden doors and discover an ancient barn that has recently been turned into a series of historical set pieces, recording the grim, and amusing, history of happenings in the house through the centuries.

During Shakespeare's lifetime The Shrieves House was a tavern and one William Rogers was the landlord. His wife's nephew was Shakespeare's godson. The poet is said to have modelled his great character Falstaff on William Rogers. Earlier, the house belonged to one of King Henry VIII's archers, whose ghost, they say, is one of many haunting the area. Visitors are reputed to have experienced the touch or feel of several different ghostly hands as they looked into the Haunted Chamber, the Witches' Glade, Falstaff's Tavern and the Tenement.
Open: daily 10.30–17.30
Entry: under £5
Tel: 01789 298070
Website: www.falstaffsexperience.co.uk
Disabled access: limited

The Gallery
Stratford Leisure Centre, Bridgefoot; map F2
A contemporary art gallery showing often innovative work by local, regional and national artists. Past exhibitions have included an attempt to harness the energy produced in the nearby gym and a look at how we create personal environments. Work on display is for sale.
Open: daily 9.00–18.00
Entry: free
Tel: 01789 414412
Disabled access: full

Country Artists

NOTHING TO WRITE HOME ABOUT

If you think there's something missing from The Gower Memorial figure of Shakespeare in Bancroft Gardens, you're right. The poet was originally shown with a quill in his hand, but the quill was stolen and replaced so often it was eventually given up as a bad job.

The Gower Memorial
Bancroft Gardens; map F3

Dilettante, sculptor and writer Lord Ronald Sutherland Gower made this huge sculpture of Shakespeare, surrounded by four of his strongest characters, in 1888. You can't miss it. The playwright is seated high above his creations – Hamlet, Lady Macbeth, Prince Hal and Falstaff – who represent the philosophic, tragic, historic and comic elements of his work.

Guild Chapel
Chapel Street; map C4

The Guild of the Holy Cross, to which most of Stratford's influential merchants and businessmen belonged, built a chapel here in 1269. Some of the present chapel, which is still used most days by the King Edward VI Grammar School next door, is original; the nave and tower are 15th century, funded by town benefactor Hugh Clopton. The glorious wall paintings were painted over during the Reformation, when the Chapel became the property of the local authority. Now some have been 'rescued' and can be seen by visitors. There's a Day of Judgement painting (known as 'Doom') over the chancel arch, and others on the west wall showing St Thomas Becket and St George.

Open: daily; Thu–Tue 9.45–16.15, Wed 11.00–16.15. (May be closed occasionally for special services)
Entry: free – there's a donations box inside
Tel: 01789 204671
Disabled access: full

HIDDEN FOR POSTERITY

Those Reformation spoilsports who decreed that churches and chapels should be plain and unadorned were sometimes responsible for preserving that which they sought to destroy. Many medieval wall paintings such as those in the Guild Chapel were protected by the covering of paint which hid them.

Guildhall and Grammar School
Church Street; map C4

On the upper floor of the Guildhall is the schoolroom, where Shakespeare would have learned Latin and maths, grammar, logic and rhetoric. It still exists pretty much as in his day and is used as a classroom by the boys of King Edward VI School. In Shakespeare's day, around 40 boys, ranging in age from 7 to 14, would have been taught in the schoolroom.

Open: occasionally open to the public – to discover the rare open days, email the school or look at their website
Email: info@likesnail.org.uk
Website: www.likesnail.org.uk

Hall's Croft
Old Town; map C5

This is the grandest and most substantial of all the houses owned and looked after by the Shakespeare Birthplace Trust. Shakespeare's elder daughter, Susanna, (whose conception in 1582 was the cause of her parents' hasty marriage) eventually married an eminent physician, Dr John Hall. The wedding was in 1607 and they occupied this lovely house whose garden contains a formal herb bed growing many of the medicinal plants actually mentioned in John Hall's medical notebooks.

Besides the beautifully looked-after period furniture and paintings, there's a room furnished as a 17th-century consulting chamber, giving some idea of how both doctors and their patients conducted their relationships 400 years ago. Other rooms include a handsome parlour, bedrooms and a large kitchen

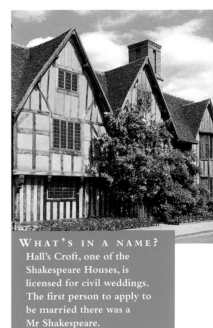

WHAT'S IN A NAME?
Hall's Croft, one of the Shakespeare Houses, is licensed for civil weddings. The first person to apply to be married there was a Mr Shakespeare.

with an enormous fireplace. If you're thinking of getting hitched, you can do it here. Hall's Croft is licensed for weddings (inquiries: 01789 201808).

Open: daily; opening times vary – ring to check
Entry: under £5. You can buy tickets which admit you to some or all of the Shakespeare properties – see page 8 for details
Tel: 01789 292107
Website: www.shakespeare.org.uk
Disabled access: limited
Other facilities: light refreshments and gift shop

Hall's Croft

Harvard House and the Museum of British Pewter
High Street; map D3

The ornate carving on the exterior timbers of this wonderful old house stops many people in their tracks as they walk along the High Street. The house (built 1596) has an interesting history, once belonging to Katherine Rogers, the mother of John Harvard – the man who financed the founding of Harvard University in America.

Although Harvard House now belongs to the American university, it is managed and cared for by the Shakespeare Birthplace Trust and contains an impressive collection of pewter, spanning 2,000 years. The display, which has many items used in religious and secular rituals in Britain, is based on the nationally important Neish Collection. The exhibits trace the use of pewter from Roman times until today. On the top floor is an interactive children's area where youngsters can have fun learning all about pewter and even have a go at making it.

Open: Easter–end Oct; days and times vary – ring to check
Entry: under £5
Tel: 01789 204016 or 01789 204507
Disabled access: limited

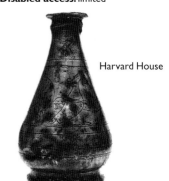

Harvard House

Holy Trinity Church
Old Town; map C6/D6

The attractions here for many people are the graves of William Shakespeare and members of his family, but even without these distinguished tombs, this is a church well worth visiting. Its peaceful setting on the banks of the Avon is part of its charm. Only when you enter, approaching the north door down a wide path lined with lime trees, do you realize how large the church is.

The church was built in the 13th and 14th centuries and is well proportioned with a wide nave, made of limestone from the Cotswold Hills. The pillars, arches and clerestory windows, all in the Perpendicular style, were built between 1280 and 1480. Most visitors make a beeline for the chancel, to search out Shakespeare's tomb.

Look carefully as you walk down the nave towards the chancel, and you will see it is skewed a little to the north. This is not uncommon – it's known as a 'weeping chancel' and is meant to suggest the angle of Christ's head on the Cross. The stained glass is nearly all Victorian – the medieval windows were destroyed in the Reformation.

DON'T MISS

Shakespeare's tomb. His place of honour in the chancel is not due to his prowess as a playwright – but to him being a lay rector of the church. Nearby, in a niche on the wall, is a carved likeness of the poet. You will be asked to pay a small sum to see the tomb and those of his family.

The carvings on the misericords (the 'mercy' ledges on the choir stalls, allowing the elderly or infirm to sit during long services). Look closely at these wonderful flights of medieval fancy. There are strange animals and creatures, a merman and a mermaid, and a winged monster with a nun's head and the hindquarters of a lion. There is even a domestic punch-up – an eloquent carving, showing a woman pulling a chap's beard while managing to hit him with a saucepan and kick him in the most painful way possible.

The altar, Holy Trinity Church

The Bible on display in the chancel. This is one of the first editions of the King James authorized version, printed in London in 1611, and the one used in the church during Shakespeare's lifetime. You'll see that it's chained – it was stolen in 1984, but quickly recovered and restored to the place where it had rested, undisturbed, for 350 years.

The ancient knocker on the inner door of the porch. It's a 13th-century sanctuary ring, giving protection for 37 days to any fugitive who reached it.

The battered and broken stone font in the chancel near Shakespeare's tomb. Not in use now, this is very likely to have been the one in which the infant William was baptized.

The magnificent tomb of George Carew, Baron Clopton, and his wife Joyce. This is in the Clopton Chapel (sometimes called the Lady Chapel), where you'll find monuments to other members of the Clopton family.

Open: daily; Mar–Oct: Mon–Sat 8.30–18.00, Sun 14.00–17.00; Nov–Feb: Mon–Sat 9.00–16.00, Sun 14.00–17.00. The church may be closed if there are special services or concerts

Entry: free, but you are asked for £1 (50p for students and concessions) to see Shakespeare's tomb and there is a church donations box

Tel: 01789 266316

Website: www.stratford-upon-avon.org
Disabled access: full
Other facilities: gift shop

Misericords, Holy Trinity Church

MYSTERY BURIAL
You'll see the graves of Shakespeare, his wife and his elder daughter Susanna in Holy Trinity Church. There is no memorial to Hamnet, his son who died at the age of 11 or to his younger daughter, Hamnet's twin, Judith, who lived until the ripe old age of 77. No one knows where they are buried.

Mary Arden's House

Mary Arden's House and the Shakespeare Countryside Museum

Wilmcote, 3 miles from the town centre along A3400

For many years, Palmer's Farm in the pretty village of Wilmcote, just outside Stratford, was thought to be the family home of Mary Arden, Shakespeare's mother. Later research showed that she was actually brought up at nearby Glebe Farm, a working farm until as recently as 1960. Both properties now belong to the Shakespeare Birthplace Trust. Glebe Farm (known as Mary Arden's House) is, in essence, a memorial to the families who have lived and worked here since the 16th century and Palmer's Farm is an interesting and lively museum.

The Tudor character of Mary Arden's home is retained, although the rooms are furnished with items that were used in the late 19th and early 20th centuries. The farm museum aims to bring to life the work and country crafts of Shakespeare's time. There is a dovecote, a forge, stables and rare breeds of animals, including Gloucester Old Spot pigs, Cotswold sheep and longhorn cattle. You can also take a walk around the farm (marked 'field walk'). If you're looking for a venue for a children's party, no problem – they'll organize it for you.

Open: daily; opening times vary – ring to check

Entry: around £5. You can buy tickets which admit you to some or all of the Shakespeare properties – see page 8 for details

Tel: 01789 293455

Website: www.shakespeare.org.uk

Disabled access: limited in the houses, full outside

Other facilities: light refreshments, picnic area and adventure playground

Falconry at
Palmer's Farm

der Mill, Palmer's Farm

Montpellier Gallery
Chapel Street; map C3
This long-established gallery shows a
wide range of crafts from glass making
to jewellery, ceramics, print making and
much more. Montpellier represents
more than 300 artists and craftsmen
and craftswomen, attracts collectors
from home and abroad and has several
solo or themed shows each year.
Open: Mon–Sat 9.30–17.30
Entry: free
Tel: 01789 261161
Website: www.montpelliergallery.com
Disabled access: full

Nash's House and New Place
Chapel Street; map C4
All you can see of New Place, the 'pretty
house of brick and timber' built originally
by Hugh Clopton for his own use and
purchased by Shakespeare a century
later for £60 in May 1597, are the foun-

dations. The financial ability to buy one
of the most substantial properties in the
town showed that the playwright, at the
age of 33, had done very well. It also
showed that, despite his success, he still
regarded Stratford as his home. He died
at New Place in 1616 after celebrating
too well, says legend, with the poets Ben
Jonson and Michael Drayton. He left the
house and its large gardens to his daughter, Susanna, and her husband. Next door
is Nash's House, which belonged to
Thomas Nash, a wealthy property
owner who married the girl next door,
Elizabeth, Shakespeare's granddaughter
and the daughter of Susanna and John.

New Place was demolished in 1759
when the then owner lost patience with
the hordes of tourists who came to
stare at it. A knot garden, based on an
Elizabethan design, now covers some of
the site, and is reached through Nash's

New Place

House. There is no charge to enter the Great Garden, which is reached by way of a gateway in Chapel Lane and which is the setting for some inspiring sculpture by American artist Greg Wyatt. Nash's House itself is well furnished and interesting, in that the upper floor contains a museum showing a lot about Stratford before and after Shakespeare's time.

Open: daily; opening times vary – ring to check

Entry: under £5. You can buy tickets which admit you to some or all of the Shakespeare properties – see page 8 for details

Tel: 01789 292325

Website: www.shakespeare.org.uk

Disabled access: limited

Ragdoll Shop

Chapel Street; map D3

Where do Rosie and Jim and the Teletubbies live? Can you enter their world? You can if you're not too big to sit in a replica of Rosie and Jim's boat.

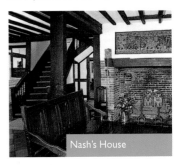

Nash's House

Hall's Croft

SWEET SWAN OF AVON
It was Shakespeare's friend and fellow-writer Ben Jonson who coined this phrase in the eulogy he penned as a preface to the 'First Folio' edition of the collected plays. In the same piece, Jonson ackowledges Shakespeare as 'Starre of Poets'.

Swan Theatre

Very young children can go to the Ragdoll Shop in Chapel Street and have a ride on the Noo-noo and the magic Brum car, watch videos of their favourite characters while sitting in that boat and even chat to a Teletubby or two on the phone. There's a large area given over to play inside the brightly coloured shop, which seems to attract big kids as well. And, of course, you can buy your very own playmate to take home.
Open: daily; Mon–Sat 9.30–17.30; Sun 10.30–16.30
Entry: free
Tel: 01789 404156
Website: www.ragdoll.co.uk
Disabled access: limited

Royal Shakespeare Theatre
Waterside; map E4
The first permanent theatre dedicated to performing the plays of Shakespeare was built here, on land donated by brewer Charles Flower, in 1879. The Shakespeare Memorial Theatre, as it was then called, burned down between the wars, to be replaced in 1932 by the current theatre designed by Elisabeth Scott. Not everyone likes the look of the solid, red-brick building on the banks of the Avon, although there is no quibble about the quality of the world-class performances from the Royal Shakespeare Company.

The charming Swan Theatre, with its round walls, distinctive roof and recon-structed Elizabethan stage, was built next door to the RST in 1986 and is as popular as the main theatre, if not more popular. There are plans to redevelop the theatres to create one of the world's leading centres for performance, training and education, but there should be little disruption to the theatre-going programme. Those wanting to find out more about behind-the-scenes activities at the theatre can take part in a back-stage tour (see phone number below for booking).

Open: ring box office for performance times; café-bar (called 1564) daily from 10.30 for coffee and light meals
Tel: box office 01789 403403; back-stage tours 01789 403405; information/booking line 0870 6091110
Website: www.rsc.org.uk
Disabled access: full
Other facilities: restaurant and café-bar overlooking the river, shop and on-line exhibition

Saturday 18 March
Meer Street and Lower Henley Street; map C2
If you see someone gazing intently at the pavement in these areas, the chances are they're trying to work out what's written there. On Saturday 18 March 2000, artist Janet Hodgson took a good look at ordinary events on these two Stratford

> **THIRTY-SIX OF THE BEST**
> It is thanks to two of Shakespeare's fellow-actors, John Heminge and Henry Condell, that the bulk of Shakespeare's work was neatly gathered together. Seven years after the playwright's death, his friends issued 36 plays in book form, now known as the 'First Folio'.

streets. She watched and listened to people going about their business in Meer Street and Lower Henley Street and the words and arrows sandblasted into the paving slabs ('look, mummy, my mice are running') tell us what she heard and saw. The artist's work was commissioned by local organizations to be an integral part of the pedestrianization of the two streets.

Meer Street

Shakespeare's Birthplace

Shakespeare's Birthplace and Exhibition
Henley Street; map C1–C2

This is where it all started: young William was the third of John Shakespeare and Mary Arden's eight children and the first to survive beyond infancy. Your ticket buys entry to the Shakespeare Exhibition and it's a good idea to take a careful look around before stepping across the way to the house itself. Only when you realize the rigorous nature of the teaching in the town's grammar school do you begin to understand how a boy with an ear for language, and an imagination capable of using the classical tales he would have read in Latin, developed his genius for expression and story-telling. Enforced church-going would have played a part, as the language of the Bible was also absorbed by the young Shakespeare.

There's domestic detail here too and a good picture of life in 16th-century Stratford. We learn of the Shakespeare family's fluctuating fortunes and circumstances, and of William's progress as an actor and playwright in London. His retirement and later life back in Stratford is documented too.

Shakespeare's Birthplace

A GOOD NIGHT'S SLEEP

Notice the staves either side of the bed in Shakespeare's Birthplace. These were to keep the mattresses in place. Very few people could afford a good, thick feather mattress, so they piled up layers stuffed with materials such as straw, putting the thin, comfortable feather one on top. But restless sleepers found all these mattresses tended to slip around, hence the staves.

and Nash's House. The out-of-town properties are Anne Hathaway's Cottage and Mary Arden's House (see entries in this section).

Open: daily; opening times vary – ring to check
Entry: under £10
Tel: 01789 201832
Website: www.shakespeare.org.uk
Disabled access: full for Shakespeare exhibition; limited to the Birthplace
Other facilities: gift shop

John Shakespeare, his father, was a glove maker, sometime money-lender and, at the time of William's birth in 1564, one of the town's most prosperous inhabitants. His status was acknowledged when he became Bailiff (the town's chief officer) and, later, Chief Alderman. So the house is a comfortable one, with bright wall-hangings and curtained beds. You'll see the workroom where he made his gloves and examples of the work he would have produced. As in all the Shakespeare houses, very well-informed guides are happy to answer any questions and come up with fascinating detail of 16th-century domestic life.

You can buy tickets which admit you to all five Shakespeare properties for under £15. A ticket to the three town properties is under £10. Both tickets are valid for one year from date of purchase. The other town properties are Hall's Croft

Grammar School

The Swan Fountain
Bancroft Gardens;
map E3
Two stainless-steel swans balance
gracefully atop this fountain, which was
switched on by Her Majesty the Queen
in 1996 to celebrate the 800th anniver-
sary of the granting of the charter that
effectively gave Stratford status as a
town. Sculptor Christine Lee was
commissioned to make the piece to
mark the occasion.

The Teddy Bear Museum
Greenhill Street; map B2
When pioneering aviators John Alcock
and Arthur Whitten Brown made their
historic first non-stop transatlantic flight
in 1919, they were not alone. In the
cabin of their Vickers Vimy were two
teddy bears. The teddy bear craze swept
America and Europe after President
Theodore 'Teddy' Roosevelt refused to
shoot a tethered bear, uttering the

memorable words, 'Spare the bear'.
That was in 1902 and soon toy makers
everywhere were turning out cuddly
'teddies', many of which are now collectors' items. You haven't seen teddies until
you've been to this museum which has
old ones, famous ones (the original
Paddington, Sooty, Pudsey and Fozzie
Bear), ones that have belonged to
celebrities (such as the bejewelled
bear owned by Barbara Cartland), and
simply cuddly ones. There is even a
Shakesbeare! The house itself used to
belong to King Henry VIII and is suitably
picturesque and oak-beamed.
Open: daily; Mar–Dec 9.30–18.00;
Jan–Feb 9.30–17.00
Entry: under £5
Tel: 01789 293160
Website: www.
theteddybearmuseum.com
Disabled access: limited
Other facilities: gift shop and
children's quiz

The Teddy Bear Museum

River Avon

BREATHING SPACE

The swan-speckled waters of the wide River Avon curl round the south-east borders of the small town of Stratford, while the canal continues the watery theme towards the north. The riverbank and the canal towpath provide peaceful, pleasant walks, well away from the traffic.

Foot ferry over the Avon

The Great Garden

Bancroft Gardens;
map E3

The river dominates Stratford's two largest areas of open space, Bancroft Gardens next to the Royal Shakespeare Theatre on the north bank, and the Recreation Ground on the south. The Bancroft was the name of the area where animals were once grazed. Later it was dominated by warehouses and wharves, but is now a grassy area where you can sit and watch the world and the river flow by. There's plenty of outdoor entertainment here in the summer, while moored boats sell refreshments – ice cream, sandwiches and other goodies.

Avonbank Garden;
map D5

This is the peaceful, grassy area between the theatres and Holy Trinity Church.

There's shade from ancient trees and good views of the river.

The Recreation Ground;
map E5–F6

There's parking here, a bandstand and children's playground and an easy walk into town across the Tramway Bridge. If you prefer, you can take the little foot ferry which will deposit you on the other bank by the Swan Theatre. But you may just want to stay here, feed the birds on the water and enjoy a peaceful picnic.

The Great Garden,
New Place, Chapel Lane;
map D4

Although this garden belongs to one of the Shakespeare houses, there's free entry to the public from Chapel Lane. It's a beautiful tranquil

place, enclosed by thick hedges and with views of the Swan Theatre. Many locals come to sit here to enjoy the peace and the striking sculptures of the American artist Greg Wyatt, inspired by Shakespeare's work.

The Firs Garden,
between Grove Road and Rother Street; map A4/B4

Another haven of tranquillity, named after a house that once stood here. The land was bought and given to the town by novelist Marie Corelli.

Memorial Garden,
Old Town; map C6

This tiny garden, near Holy Trinity Church, is a tribute to the people of Stratford who died in the service of their country. There are plenty of benches and it's a good place for a peaceful ten minutes.

Ice cream boat

Mayfair Florists (page 60)

S H O P P I N G

A spending spree in Stratford could turn into a day-long expedition as shops and history twine comfortably together. A shopping trip can become a leisurely exploration of the lanes and streets, where you'll pick up not only interesting retail reminders of your stay, but also a powerful impression of a town whose history lives today. The centre is not large and was laid out in 1196 on a neat grid system, making it easy to find your way about. This section picks out some of the many interesting shops in the main retail areas – you'll spot others as you make your way around Stratford's streets.

Opening hours
A very few shops still close early on Thursdays, but most are open seven days a week during the summer and just before Christmas. If you visit Stratford out of season, you'll find there are fewer Sunday openings.

High Street shops
The starting point for most visitors is Bridge Street with its wide road and splendid views down to the 15th-century Clopton Bridge.

A quick glance reveals many interesting old buildings – and, it appears, none of the usual high-street names. But look again and you'll see that the old familiar faces are there – in unfamiliar guise.

The identity of the buildings is stronger than the brand names, so you'll probably do a double take when you realize that it is Marks and Spencer behind the bow windows and that Boots, Smiths, Mothercare, Jaeger, Viyella, Laura Ashley, New Look, Next and the rest are not very far away.

G O S S I P S ' M A R K E T
Stratford's medieval market was held in a hall with covered arches where Barclays Bank now stands in Henley Street. This was where the farmers' wives would meet to sell their butter and cheeses – and to exchange news. It was commonly known as the 'gossips' market'.

Elaine Ripon Craft Gallery (page 60)

Mixed in with the well-known names are many independent retailers selling clothes, shoes, furnishings, arts and crafts, souvenirs and presents, bits and pieces for house and garden, flowers, chocolate, jewellery and food. The style of the shops is restrained – thankfully Stratford is not swamped with cheap Shakespeare souvenirs.

Stratford's newest shopping mall is Town Square (map C3) where you'll find many more high-street names.

Clothes shops
Old Red Lion Courtyard; map D3
Here you'll find a whole wardrobe of fashion retailers from upmarket Alexon and The Dresser to popular labels such as Kaliko, Dash, Monsoon, Phase Eight and super-cool Zip Loc. There's Daisy Chain too, with all sorts of clothes and other necessities for babies and for toddlers.

Wood Street; map C2
Gemini is a place of pilgrimage for serious clothes shoppers. There's a huge range of labels and plenty of help and advice from owner Claire Wright and her dedicated 'Gemini Girls'.

Sheep Street; map D3–E3
This small street is full of good clothes shops including Loxleys and Prima (and Prima Shoes too), Ideal Clothes, Madeleine Ann, Anne Tudor and Basler at No. 20.

Shrieves Walk; map D3
Another good hunting ground for fashion with Bali Balo, Beautique and Prima Donna.

High Street; map D3
Rohde Shoes are at
No. 16, while you need
to make for Cook's Alley
(map C2) to discover
Gemini Shoes.

Food shops
Bread
Meer Street; map C2

Look for Havilands inde-
pendent bakers for a good
range of delicious breads
and other goods.

Cheese
Wood Street; map C2
'A gentleman buys his
cheese only from Paxton
and Whitfield,' said

Winston Churchill. You'll
find this old-established,
family cheesemonger's
shop full of enticing and
mouth-watering goodies.

Delicatessen
The Minories; map C2
Martini's Deli has a good
range of delicatessen food
– ideal for picnics by the
river on a sunny day.

Chocolates
Henley Street; map C1
You'll find yourself press-
ing your nose against the
window of Truffles, inde-
pendent chocolatiers
(since 1910), who supply

**MEET THE TELETUBBIES
AND FRIENDS**
Ragdoll Productions is the company which
makes children's TV programmes such as
Rosie and Jim, *Teletubbies* and *Tots TV*. Ragdoll
is their toy shop in Chapel Street, where
youngsters can meet their favourite characters and play in the boats and cars.

Truffles

Winnie the Pooh chess set here), is much photographed for the original beauty of the building.

Pewter
The Tappit Hen has a window gleaming with English pewter in the shape of spoons, bowls, plates, jewellery, models and tappit hens (drinking flagons) themselves.

Shakespearean gifts and books
It's in Henley Street that you'll find The Shakespeare Shop and The Shakespeare Bookshop, near the poet's birthplace. They sell quality gifts and books.

Wild and Woolly
This shop sells – you've guessed it – soft toys.

and make chocolate heaven. If you long for the sherbet dabs and pear drops of your childhood, visit their other establishment, The Little Sweet Shop, just up the road.

Gifts
Henley Street; map C1–C2
Henley Street is the main place for gifts. It is, after all, where Shakespeare was born. Look for Browsers, Presents in Mind, The House of Green and The Crystal Shop.

Model characters
The Birthplace is a beautiful half-timbered house – but it's not the only one. Gilmers gift shop, with its amazing collection of model characters from fiction (you can buy a

Waterside; map E4
Swan Theatre and RST
The Royal Shakespeare Company's two shops have a huge range of souvenirs – from T-shirts, mugs and books to pencils, scarves and jigsaw puzzles. They're well worth a visit for a present with a difference.

Bard's Walk; map C2
Here you'll find the Castle

The Shakespeare Shop

Gilmers (page 58)

Gemini (page 56)

Gallery and Once a Tree, selling (that's right) wooden souvenirs.

The Minories; map C2
In this courtyard off Henley Street you'll find the Elaine Ripon Craft Gallery with the most lovely textiles, contemporary paintings, ceramics, glass and crafts from British designers.

Homes and gardens
Meer Street; map C2
Vinegar Hill is a classy gift and home furnishing shop with furniture, china and lots of good ideas. It's owned by the family who run Havilands, the bakers a few doors away. Nearby, the AGA shop is a cook's paradise, while a visit to Garden Images, who stock not only practical but also attractive garden accessories, could give even non-gardeners ideas.

Greenhill Street; map B2
Here you'll find many different kinds of shops. Kitchenalia is a useful-looking cooks' shop, while nearby Stephen Ramm Fabrics displays richly coloured furnishing materials. The family-run Pine Centre has well-designed kitchen and bathroom furniture, while Mayfair Florist sell their lovely flowers from another charming Tudor building.

Rother Street; map B2
For those who like their home comforts and classy decorations, Atelier is the place to visit for furnishings just that little bit out of the ordinary. You will also find a range of household paints here.

Wild and Woolly (page 59)

S OF GRACE
~ and ANNE
we to
AND WOOLLY
~00 each.
OR
50-00
ThePair

ONLY TO
WILD AND WOOLLY

CHEQUERED HISTORY

The building occupied by Crabtree and Evelyn on the corner of the High Street was once a gaol with an outside cage where prisoners had to suffer jeers and abuse from passers-by. It was later the home of Judith, Shakespeare's younger daughter.

Vinegar Hill (page 60)

Henley Street; map C1–C2

Traditional china is sold in Lamberts, while the Stratford Craft and Woollens Centre is a large shop crammed with materials for every craft and hobby imaginable, and probably some you've never heard of.

Wood Street; map C2

Every town should have a kitchenware shop and ironmongers that sells everything. Those in the know say that Lacey and Sons is one such shop.

Books and antiques
Henley Street; map C1–C2

Head for The Shakespeare Bookshop for books about and by you-know-who. A general list is

carried by The Works, not far away. The Antique Shop is at No. 30.

Bridge Street; map D2–E2

More Shakespeare and other good books can be had in Mahers The Bookseller, housed in a fine, old, half-timbered building in Bridge Street.

Chapel Street; map C3–D3

Not too far from each other are the Chaucer Head and Robert Vaughan bookshops.

Ely Street; map C3

This ancient street, with timber-framed houses restored to their original colour, is the place to hunt for antiques. Apart from Lovejoy Antiques – yes, really – and Queen Anne

Antiques and Crafts, the Ely Street Antiques Market has more than 50 small shops to spend time trawling through.

The Minories; map C2

The Loquens Gallery stocks paintings, antique prints and postcards.

Other specialist shops
Traditional tobacconist
Henley Street; map C2

Remember when every town had a proper tobacconist, with tins piled up high, racks of pipes and hand-carved walking sticks? Lands on the corner of Henley Street and Cook's Alley will take you back to those days.

Jewellery
Cook's Alley; map C2

Walk up this little passageway where you can admire the contemporary jewellery in Zontal.

Toys
Windsor Street; map B2

Much Ado About Toys might be a name too far but the shop itself is a good one and the UK's top supplier of model railways. Youngsters will also enjoy Ragdoll in Chapel Street (see page 61).

Garden Images (page 60)

Atelier (page 60)

Jester statue, Henley Street

Markets

There's a Friday street market in Rother Street (map B3), the town's original marketplace. The ever-popular Farmers' Market is also held in Rother Market on two Saturdays every month (see page 84).

Out of town

The Country Artists Visitor Centre and factory shop at Avenue Farm (see page 36) is a big draw and a good place to buy a souvenir, while antique hunters make a beeline for Stratford Antiques and Interiors Centre about 2 miles out of town on the Dodwell Trading Estate, Evesham Road.

The Hatton Country World near Warwick is a large shopping outlet combined with an adventure farm park, while Yew Tree Farm Craft Centre at Wootton Wawen, near Henley-in-Arden, is a farmyard conversion selling country crafts.

JESTER OF FRIENDSHIP

The carefree jester dancing on his plinth at the end of Henley Street was made by sculptor James Butler RA, and given in 1994 by Stratford man Anthony Bird OBE as a 'token of esteem' for the town which had given him so much pleasure and friendship.

EATING AND DRINKING

Music may be the food of love, but even in Stratford you need something a little more substantial to keep body and soul together. Although Stratford is a small town it has an impressive number of restaurants, cafés and pubs. There are excellent eateries both in the town and in nearby villages. You'll find a good range of food, from family-run Italian to Thai with a view.

Benson's (page 66)

One experience you shouldn't miss is a trip on Nick and Lisa Longden's boat-restaurant, *The Countess of Evesham*. In both summer and winter you can book lunch or dinner (modern English cooking) and a cruise on the River Avon from her moorings in the Canal Basin, opposite the Royal Shakespeare Theatre. For details see page 69.

Many of the restaurants offer post-theatre meals – so that you can eat after a production at the Royal Shakespeare Theatre. See the section headed 'post-theatre' on page 72.

The Brasserie (page 70)

SPECIALS

Roast Loin of Pork with sage & onion stuffing, apple sauce, new & roast potatoes & todays fresh veg, or baked potato with sour cream and salad   £6.95

Cottage Pie-minced beef in gravy topped with creamy mashed potato, served with fresh veggies   £6.95

Roast Chicken with sage & onion stuffing, new & roast potatoes & todays fresh veggies, or baked potato with sour cream and salad   £6.95

'Lashfords' prize winning pork & leek sausages on 'bubble & squeak' with daddies sauce   £5.95

Spinach & Ricotta Tortellini in a tomato sauce served with garlic bread & salad garnish   £6.95

Club sandwich served with salad garnish & crisps   £5.95

Baguette served with todays roast with salad garnish & crisps   £5.95

CAFES
Bard's Walk; map C2
Benson's calls itself a café but it's more than just a coffee shop. Breakfasts can include croissants, scrambled eggs, muffins and smoked bacon, while you could find a delicious fish platter, home-made savoury tarts and good soups for lunch. Patisserie features large in their afternoon teas.

Bridge Street; map D2
We've grown accustomed to Costa Coffee but, as with many old familiar faces in Stratford, it comes heavily disguised in an old, half-timbered building in Bridge Street.

Greenhill Street; map B2
Try coffee and a bite to eat at the tiny Bruno's Bakery, convenient if you are this way visiting The Teddy Bear Museum.

Henley Street; map C2
Drucker's Vienna Patisserie in Henley Street will keep you well fed. If you happen to be over the other side of Stratford in Old Town (map C5), you will find Drucker's have another coffee shop at Hall's Croft.

Havilands (page 69)

Cream Tea £3.95
2 Slices Toast £1.20.
2 Slices Chunky
   Toast £1.40.
Breakfast Baguette.
with jam, honey or
marmalade
   £1.50.

TRAY BAKES

Flapjack   Choc Caramel
Toffee Mallow   Walnut Slice
Shortbread   Ginger Latte
Eccles   Coconut Custard
                Danish

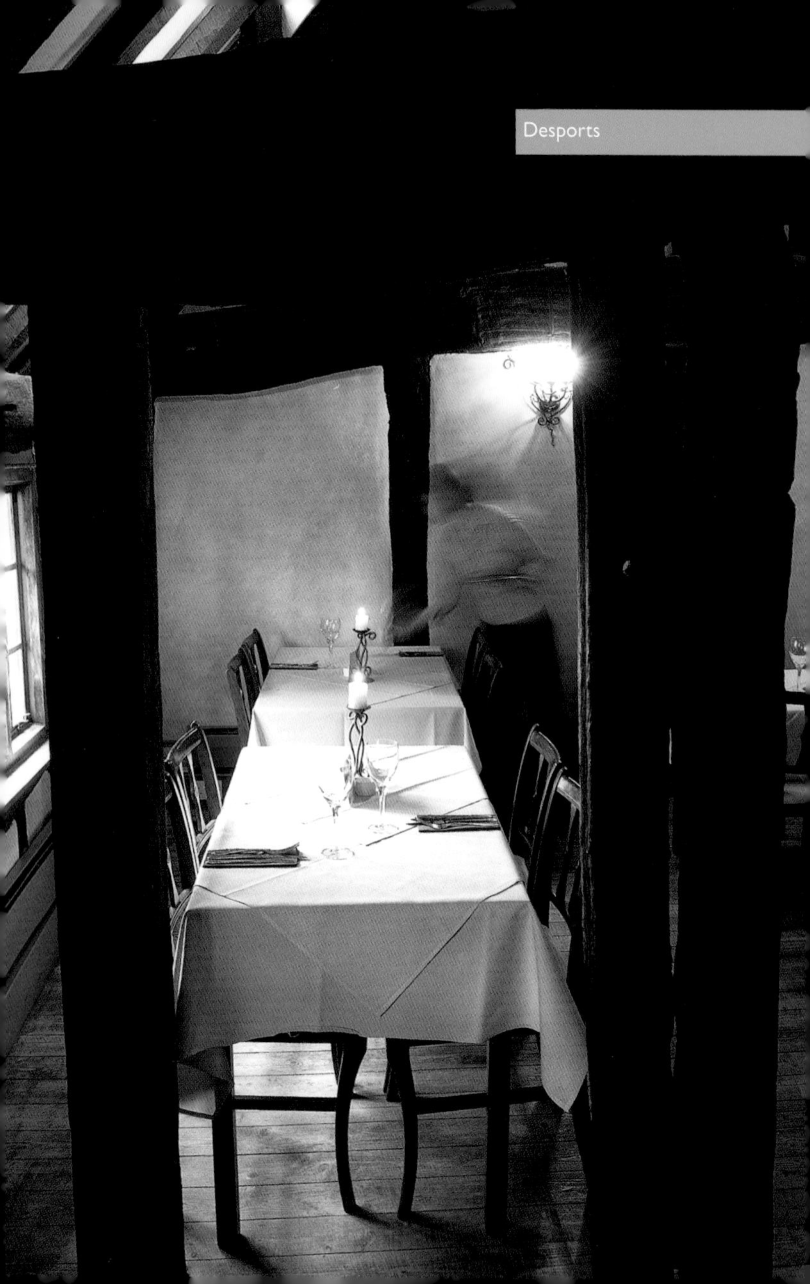

The Brasserie on Henley Street leaves you in no doubt about its location. It's in a good situation for afternoon tea (you must try the cream scones) or a snack, as it's just across the road from Shakespeare's Birthplace.

Meer Street; map C2

Look for Havilands café in Meer Street (owned by the bakers of the same name) where you'll be offered good things to eat with your coffee.

Waterside; map E4

They do a good cup of coffee, and light meals too, at 1564 – the Royal Shakespeare Theatre's café-bar, on the banks of the River Avon.

CELEBRATING FOOD

Many Stratford restaurants take part in the new Festival of Food and Drink in September when visitors can enjoy cookery demonstrations, wine tastings, food sampling sessions and special festival 'meal deals'.

TAKEAWAY SANDWICHES

Chadds
Union Street; map D2
'Handcrafted' sandwiches is the proud boast here.

Martini's Deli
The Minories; map C2
Delicious freshly made takeouts on baguettes or ciabatta bread.

Munchies
Meer Street; map C2
Large selection of equally large sandwiches.

RESTAURANTS

The list below is not exhaustive but will give you some idea of what's on offer in and around Stratford. It's best to ring ahead to book and check opening times.

Chinese
China Garden
21 Windsor Street; map B1–C1
Good Cantonese food served in pleasant surroundings. Takeaway available too.
Tel: 01789 293009

Mayflower
22a High Street; map D3
Traditional Chinese restaurant in the heart of the town. Also takeaway.
Tel: 01789 297161

Ripple Café
Swan's Nest Lane; map F4
Very good place to eat before the theatre; they do a delicious oriental buffet that should sustain you through the longest performance.
Tel: 01789 292121

English/global cooking
The Countess of Evesham, **boat-restaurant**
Canal Basin; map E3
Modern English food with a fine river view, summer and winter (there's central heating on board). Lunch departures are at 12.30 (return at 14.00) while dinner cruise lasts from 19.30–22.30.
Tel: 01789 293477

Desports
13–14 Meer Street; map C2
This ancient, half-timbered building houses a first-floor restaurant where the food is divided into 'sections' – earth, land, sea and heaven (puddings come from heaven). Menu examples include fragrant duck breast in five spice with sesame greens and sweet potato, lentil and

Margaux

chickpea cakes, and pork and chorizo terrine. They do a good tarte Tatin.
Tel: 01789 269304

Edward Moon Brasserie
9 Chapel Street; map C3
Lively atmosphere and well-cooked food with a good range of meat and fish dishes – and recom-mended puddings.
Tel: 01789 267069

Embargo
Guild Street; map C1
One of Stratford's newest restaurants, under the same ownership as the Fox and Goose pub at nearby Armscote.
Tel: 01789 262233

Lambs
12 Sheep Street; map D3
Another good, reliable eatery, offering set-price and à la carte menus in one of the oldest buildings in Stratford.
Tel: 01789 292554

Margaux
6 Union Street; map D2
Colourful bistro offering imaginative cooking with a Mediterranean feel. Run by husband and wife team Shaun and Maggie Brebner, the bistro offers delicious dishes such as lobster and langoustine terrine, and roast quail with seasonal vegetables.
Tel: 01789 269106

Marlowe's Restaurant
18 High Street; map D3
Traditional silver-service restaurant, a favourite with actors. In its oak-panelled dining room Marlowe's serves mouth-watering dishes such as asparagus and tarragon ravioli.
Tel: 01789 204999

The Opposition

The Opposition
13 Sheep Street; map D3
'The Oppo' is a favourite
with locals and theatre-
goers alike. It serves good
bistro-style food.
Tel: 01789 269980

Quartos
Royal Shakespeare
Theatre; map E4
The RSC restaurant is
open for pre- and post-
performance meals and
for lunch when there's a
matinée. Apart from the
good quality of food you
can enjoy wonderful views
across the river.
Tel: 01789 403415

Russons
8 Church Street; map C4
Friendly bistro serving
good Caesar salad, grilled
silver dorade with basil
oil, and puddings such as
banoffi pie.
Tel: 01789 268822

Vintner's Bistro
5 Sheep Street; map D3
As you'd expect from the
name, the wine list is
good here and the food
is bistro-style.
Tel: 01789 297259

Fish and Chips
Barnaby's Fish Bar
Waterside; map E3
Wonderful fish and chips
at Barnaby's next to the
theatre. In summer you
can munch them in
nearby Bancroft Gardens.

Indian
The Coconut Lagoon
21 Sheep Street; map D3
Specializing in southern
Indian dishes, the Coconut
Lagoon comes up with
imaginative and nicely
served food such as
crunchy papads, Nizan
pepper chicken and
Goanese curry.
Tel: 01789 293546

Laghbagh
3a Greenhill Street;
map B2
If you long for tandoori
food, this is just the place
for you.
Tel: 01789 293563

Raj
7 Greenhill Street; map B2
Traditional Indian restaurant food.
Tel: 01789 267067

Thespians
Sheep Street; map D3
Indian with a touch of
theatricals in the name.
Bangladeshi, Northern
Indian, Tandoori and Balti
dishes are specialities.
Tel: 01789 295279

Usha Indian Cuisine
28 Meer Street; map C2
Reliable Indian food.
Tel: 01789 297348

Italian
Café Pasta
Sheep Street; map D3
Upmarket offshoot of
Pizza Express (you'll find
PE in Ely Street). Good
service and menu in a
lovely old building.
Tel: 01789 262910

Caffé Uno
22 Wood Street; map C2
A better-than-most Italian
chain of restaurants with
good service and range of
Italian food.
Tel: 01789 414494

Sorrento Restaurant
8 Ely Street; map C3
Vito Ferro and his family
run this most comfortable
of restaurants on tradi-
tional lines with silver
service and well-cooked
Italian food.
Tel: 01789 297999

Malaysian
Georgetown
23 Sheep Street; map D3
Colonial Malaysian food
(choose from Malay,
Mandarin or Tamil dishes)
is what they do here,
preceded by a refreshing
Singapore Sling.
Tel: 01789 204445

Post theatre
The following restaurants
all offer 'post-RSC' meals:
Café Pasta, Caffé Uno,
Georgetown, Marlowe's,
The Opposition, Quarto
at the RSC, Sorrento,
Thai Boathouse.
Some of the Indian and
Chinese restaurants stay
open until midnight; check
when booking.

Thai
Thai Boathouse
Swan's Nest Lane; map F4
Elegant restaurant serving
lovely food in beautiful
surroundings. Overlooking
the River Avon and near
the theatre, this restaurant
offers the bonus of good
food in a very pleasant
atmosphere.
Tel: 01789 297733

Thai Kingdom
11 Warwick Road;
map E1
More good Thai food.

The Coconut Lagoon (page 71)

Soup of the day £3.50
Moules Mariniere £5.50
Pan-fried Sardines with lemon + parsley butter £4.75

Smoked haddock, prawn + spinach crepes glazed
with parmesan £8.95
Pork + chive Sausages with leek mash + whole-
grain mustard sauce £8.95
Saute of fillet Steak "Strognoff" with basmati
rice £11.25
Pan-fried whole lemon sole with prawn + caper butter
Served with green beans + new potatoes £13.50

The Opposition (page 71)

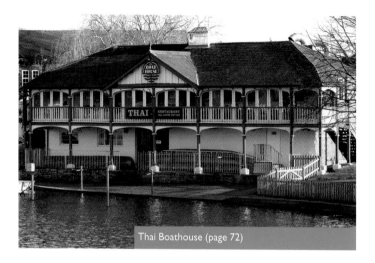
Thai Boathouse (page 72)

PUBS

Cross Keys
Ely Street; map C3
Lively feel to this pub
that attracts lots of young
people in the evenings.

The Dirty Duck
Waterside; map D4
Theatrical and friendly, the
DD (or The Black Swan
as it's properly called)
attracts actors and their
public with its good beer,
food and pretty location.

Falcon
Chapel Street; map C3
Huge, half-timbered Tudor
building that is home to
a pub and a hotel. Good
range of bar food.

The Garrick Inn
High Street; map D3
So Stratford it looks like
a cliché. The heavily half-
timbered building is full of
nooks and crannies. It was

named in 1769 when
actor David Garrick came
here to open the Stratford
Festival. The pub serves
well-kept beer and good
quality food.

The Dirty Duck

Pen and Parchment

Pen and Parchment
Bridgefoot; map E2
A touch of the Bard here with its flagstones, boards and big open fire. Reliable food and beer. Good service, too.

Slug and Lettuce
Guild Street; map D1
This large, bustling bar serves food all day and provides newspapers for customers to read. Children are welcomed.

The Windmill Inn
Church Street; map C4
Lovely unpretentious old pub with no gimmicks. Open fires, low beams, good value food and well-kept beer.

OUT OF TOWN
There are many good restaurants and pubs just a few miles away. Here is a selection:

Edmunds
64 High Street, Henley-in-Arden
Restaurant in a half-timbered house that is run by a husband and wife team. Good, modern English cooking that features fresh ingredients, such as Scotch beef, hake and Loch Fyne salmon. Tel: 01564 795666

Fox and Goose Inn
Arsmcote; off the A3400 Stratford–Shipston road
Once a blacksmith's forge, but now a pub that has been handsomely done up. There's a restaurant as well as bar food.

The Windmill Inn

A MEAL WITH A VIEW

Book a lunch or dinner cruise on *The Countess of Evesham* (see page 69) or a table at the Thai Boathouse (see page 72) for a meal with added interest. Or simply buy fish and chips at Barnaby's near the Waterside (see page 71) and sit by the river to enjoy them.

The Dirty Duck (page 74)

Imaginative dishes include Thai chicken on a coconut risotto cake, and seared razor clams with home-made linguini and red and yellow pepper sauce.
Tel: 01608 682293

Howard Arms
Ilmington; off A3400 south of Stratford
Honey-coloured inn with well-cooked, interesting bar and restaurant food. Dishes could include fried skate with lemon, capers and gingered pear and brandy; scallops with garlic and parsley butter; chocolate and ginger tart. Pretty garden and pleasant, friendly service.
Tel: 01608 682226

White Bear
High Street, Shipston-on-Stour; A3400 south of Stratford
Bar and restaurant food with tempting dishes such as fried pigeon breast with pine kernels; garlic and parsley, grilled brill with anchovy butter and rocket; baked cheesecake with plum sauce. Comfortable and nicely furnished, too.
Tel: 01608 661558

The Shakespeare Hotel, Chapel Street

AN EVENING OUT

The honeyed words and subtle plots of William Shakespeare are what lure many of us to Stratford, so it's only natural that, having spent the day exploring his town and historic houses, we should want to watch some of the country's best actors performing his works in the evening.

A night at the theatre
Take your pick. The Stratford theatres are undergoing reorganization, but the play's still the thing. The two theatres – the monolithic Royal Shakespeare Theatre and the distinctive and popular

Marlowe's Restaurant and Hathaway Tearooms

Margaux (page 70)

Swan – both have packed and varied programmes. If Shakespeare's not your thing, there is also comedy, other drama, dance or light opera to choose from. See page 47 for booking details.

Other entertainment
Music, drama and entertainment is on offer throughout the year at Stratford's Civic Hall in Rother Street (map B3). Why not pick up a programme at the Tourist Information Centre (see page 94) or ring the Civic Hall on 01789 269332?

Eating and drinking
You can hang out with the actors at The Dirty Duck or go olde worlde at The Garrick Inn, or eat out as the fancy takes you – Stratford has a good range of restaurants, including some high-street names but also some excellent individual eating houses. See pages 65–76.

Be very scared
'Witches and ghosts and things not right …' – that's what the weekly Stratford ghost walk is all about. Guide John Hogg is a magician too, so be prepared for surprises on your evening perambulation of the scariest bits of the town. You'll hear about (and perhaps see) the ghostly goings-on in Sheep Street, Marlowe's Restaurant and the Hathaway Tearooms among other haunted places. The walk starts at 19.30 each Thursday at The Swan Fountain, in Bancroft Gardens (map E3). You can simply turn up, or ring 01789 292478 or 07855 760377 for details. It costs under £5 for an adult.

Cinema and other performances
Check out the Picture House in Windsor Street (map B2) for the latest films (ring 01789 415511 for information) and the Tourist Information Centre (see page 94) for details of other entertainment. Look at pages 84–85 for information about regular events and festivals.

Royal Shakespeare Theatre

TOURS AND TRIPS

You can see Stratford and its surrounds on foot, by boat, by bus and even by steam train. Here are some ideas for a different view of the town.

On the water

The River Avon can be explored by boat. Trips last around half an hour and take place between April and the end of October. Avon Boating has its base in Bancroft Gardens (map E3) next to the theatre. Simply turn up and board. If you fancy going it alone, hire a canoe, punt or rowing boat from the opposite bank of the river. Tel: 01789 267073 for details or party bookings.

Bancroft Cruisers offer similar sightseeing cruises. They depart from the Moat House Hotel wharf (map F3). They're also available for charter. Tel: 01789 269669

Open-top bus

Sightseeing tours on colourful open-top buses leave the Pen and Parchment by the Tourist Information Centre (map F2) and Cox's Yard (map

Narrow boat on the Avon

Rowing boats for hire

F3) at regular intervals. They visit the Shakespeare houses and other places of interest. A ticket lasts for 24 hours and you may hop on and off as often as you like. Choose a live guided tour or a taped commentary (choice of seven languages and a commentary for children). Ring 01789 294466 for details

Behind the scenes
If you'd like to see behind the glamour and the greasepaint at the Royal Shakespeare Theatre, you can book a backstage tour. Book in advance on 01789 403405.

Shakespeare Express
This steam locomotive runs between Stratford and Birmingham every Sunday from July until the beginning of September, departing from Stratford railway station off Alcester Road (map A2). Journeys last one hour each way. Tel: 0121 707 4696 for details

A day at the races
Stratford Racecourse, a five-minute drive from the town centre, offers regular meetings, plus family days and events.
Tel: 01789 267949 for details

Stratford on foot
An insider's glimpse is given by professional guides who will walk you gently around Stratford, revealing its history and secrets. Simply turn up at The Swan Fountain, Bancroft Gardens (map E3) Mon–Fri at 11.00, Sat and Sun at 14.00 (no walks during the last week of December).
Tel: 01789 292478 or 07855 760377 for details

Guide Link will supply a 'tailor-made' professional Blue Badge guide for your particular needs, and provides guides for individuals and groups.
Tel: 01789 772786

Jo de la Mare is a Blue Badge guide who specializes in Stratford-upon-Avon, Warwick and the Cotswold towns and provides commentaries and walking tours for large or small groups.
Tel: 01926 496077

David Maine is another professional tour guide also specializing in Stratford, Warwick and the Cotswolds.
Tel: 01527 500865

> **MAKING THEIR MARK**
> In the past some of Stratford's visitors were less well-behaved than those today. Take a look at the large window in Shakespeare's Birthplace where 19th-century visitors scratched their signatures – there are some famous names amongst them.

Stratford has its own calendar of performing arts, shows and festivals and is only a few miles from Warwick and Leamington Spa where there are more events. The nearby National Agricultural Centre (NAC) at Stoneleigh is used for national festivals while Ragley Hall at Alcester, six miles to the west of Stratford, is also a major venue.

WHAT'S ON

Shakespeare Birthday Celebrations

Regular events
The Orchestra of the Swan give regular concerts at the Civic Hall.
Tel: 01789 414513

Farmers' Market
Farmers' Market is held twice-monthly on Saturdays in the Rother Street marketplace.
Tel: 01789 267000

Racing
Horse racing is held regularly throughout the year at Stratford Racecourse, Luddington Road.
Tel: 01789 267949

Regular race meetings are held at Warwick Racecourse, Hampton Street, Warwick.
Tel: 01926 491553

Festivals and major events
Information on all events available from the Tourist Information Centre.
Tel: 01789 293127

January
Militaria – annual indoor military collectors' exhibition, NAC, Stoneleigh.
Tel: 01283 820050

February
Toy and Train Collectors
Fair, NAC, Stoneleigh.
Tel: 01526 398198

March
Craft Fair, Ragley Hall,
Alcester.
Tel: 01789 762090

April
Gardeners' Weekend,
Ragley Hall, Alcester.
Tel: 01789 762090

Shakespeare Birthday
Celebrations, Stratford,
including lecture, RSC
performance and charity
ball, procession, marching
bands, folk dancing and
beating the retreat.
Tel: 01789 204016

Shakespeare Birthday
Concert, Civic Hall,
Stratford.
Tel: 01789 414513

Stratford marathon
and half-marathon.
Tel: 01789 295314

May
Dragon boat racing, River
Avon and Recreation
Ground.
Tel: 01536 712831
Classic Car and Transport
Show, Ragley Hall, Alcester.
Tel: 01789 762090

June
Stratford Boat Club
regatta, River Avon and
Recreation Ground.
Tel: 01789 294692
The Royal Show, NAC,
Stoneleigh.
Tel: 02476 858285

July
The Royal Show, NAC,
Stoneleigh.
Tel: 02476 858285
Stratford International
Flute Festival, 10 Guild
Street; map D1.
Tel: 01789 261561
Stratford Poetry Festival.
Tel: 01789 292176

August
Stratford International
Flute Festival, 10 Guild
Street; map D1.
Tel: 01789 261561
Town and Country
Festival, NAC, Stoneleigh.
Tel: 02476 858285

September
Festival of Food and
Drink, Stratford.
Tel: 01455 287076
Gardeners' Weekend,
Ragley Hall, Alcester.
Tel: 01789 762090

October
Stratford-upon-Avon
Music Festival.
Tel 01926 496277
Craft Fair, Ragley Hall,
Alcester.
Tel: 01789 762090
Stratford Mop Fair (see
page 87).

November
Craft Fair, Ragley Hall,
Alcester.
Tel: 01789 762090

December
Candlelit tours of Ragley
Hall, Alcester.
Tel: 01789 762090

STRATFORD FOR KIDS

Don't worry if the kids groan at your passion for Shakespeare; they might change their minds once they visit the Shakespeare Exhibition and Birthplace and, even if they don't, there's plenty more to keep them happy.

Butterflies and creepy-crawlies

You'll all love the rainforest feel of the Butterfly Farm at Tramway Walk (see page 34), where you can traipse through a lush landscape spotting hundreds of exotic inhabitants. Many children will particularly like the huge spiders and scorpions in Arachnoland — home, they claim, to the world's largest spider.

Harvard House

From the outside this wonderful old building (see page 39) might not look like a whole lot of fun for kids, but get them upstairs to Pewter Power where they can play interactive computer games and make their own pewter. Downstairs is the Museum of British Pewter.

Truly scary

You might be scared, but kids will love a visit to The Shrieves House in Sheep Street for the theatrical Falstaff Experience (see page 36). A series of historical set pieces record the sometimes grim and sometimes funny history of happenings in the house. Visitors are reputed to have experienced the touch of different ghostly hands in the Haunted Chamber, the Witches' Glade, Falstaff's Tavern and the spooky Tenement.

Hands on

You can produce your own memento of your visit to the Stratford Brass Rubbing Centre (see page 34), where they'll show you what to do and, for a small charge (depending on the size of the brass), let you get on with it.

Butterfly Farm

ALL THE FUN OF THE FAIR
If you happen to be in Stratford on the weekend nearest 12 October, prepare to enjoy yourself. The annual Mop Fair takes over the town. It's a huge funfair evolved from the time when a fair was held to hire workers and servants, who presumably held the tools of their trade (including mops) to indicate their skills.

Exit, pursued by a bear
From Paddington to Fozzie and the Bear of Avon, William Shakesbeare – you'll find them in their hundreds in this award-winning museum. The Teddy Bear Museum (see page 50) in Greenhill Street is stuffed full of enchanting toys, some famous and others rare and valuable. There's lots to see and do to keep young people occupied.

Rosie and Jim – and the rest
You won't be able to drag younger children away from the Ragdoll Shop (see page 44) in Chapel Street. Here they can meet their best-loved TV toys, watch episodes of *Rosie and Jim* and other programmes, and talk to some of their favourite characters on a special telephone hotline.

Special treats
Buy an ice cream from the boat moored on the river or take a trip on the Avon (see page 82). Check out the Royal Shakespeare Company (01789 403403) for children's shows. Enjoy a few hours in Bancroft Gardens (map E3) where there are play areas and entertainers.

Pewter Power

Brass Rubbing Centre

OUT OF TOWN

There's plenty to see and do in Stratford itself, but the surrounding countryside is full of tempting places to visit. Here are a few suggestions:

Coughton Court,
near Alcester
9 miles north-west of Stratford, via A46 to Alcester, then A435

Although this is a National Trust property it is lived in and managed by the Throckmortons, whose family home it has been since 1409. There's a lot for lovers of fine old houses and gardens to see – look for the walled garden, flower garden and bog garden. The house has substantial collections that include furniture, porcelain and paintings, as well as a gift shop and licensed restaurant.
Tel: 01789 400777 or the information line 01789 762435
Website: www.coughtoncourt.co.uk

Warwick Castle
8 miles north-east of Stratford, via A439/A429

You should allow the best part of a day to visit this massive and beautifully preserved medieval castle. Be warned – it does get very busy at peak times. Apart from the tour round the castle itself, you'll see the Kingmaker exhibition, showing Richard Neville, Earl of Warwick, preparing to do battle against Edward IV in 1471 and the armoury exhibition on the ground floor. The Mill and Engine

Coughton Court

Warwick Castle

Warwick Castle

House, now restored, was the wonder of Victorian England when, in 1894, it generated enough electricity to light up the castle. Conservatory, peacock garden, restored Victorian rose garden, icehouses, two restaurants and gift shops make this a major attraction.
Tel: 0870 442 2000 (information line)
Website: www. warwick-castle.co.uk

Wellesbourne Watermill,
Wellesbourne
6 miles east of Stratford
off B4086 from Wellesbourne to Kineton You can see how flour used to be ground in this historic mill in a very pretty setting. Sample the end result in the shape of delicious scones and cakes in the tearoom.
Tel: 01789 470237
Website: www. wellesbournemill.co.uk

Whichford Pottery,
Whichford
12 miles south of Stratford off A3400 between Shipston-on-Stour and Chipping Norton
Raw clay is transformed by hand into flowerpots of all shapes and sizes by a team of skilled craftsmen and craftswomen at this long-established and traditional pottery. There are plenty of planting ideas in the garden and you'll probably leave with a pot or two in the back of the car. There's no tearoom but good food and drink are provided at the White Bear in Shipston-on-Stour and the Chequers in Chipping Norton.
Tel: 01608 684416
Website: www. whichfordpottery.com

Hidcote Manor

The Cotswolds

Just a few miles drive south from Stratford is the Cotswolds, an area that contains some of the most picturesque and enchanting small towns and villages in the country.

Moreton-in-Marsh, Stow-on-the-Wold, Broadway, Bourton-on-the-Water and Upper and Lower Slaughter are all names to look out for. A leisurely drive around this part of Gloucestershire, with

frequent stops to explore the villages with their honey-coloured stone houses and cottages, gives a very pleasant day out.

Great Gardens

About 8 miles south of Stratford, signposted from the B4632

Two of England's most renowned gardens are within just a few miles of Stratford-upon-Avon. Hidcote, with its famous 'garden rooms', was the creation of plant collector and great horticulturist, Lawrence Johnston. Now owned by The National Trust, it's famed for rare shrubs and trees, unusual plants and wonderful

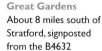

Hidcote Manor

Blenheim Palace

herbaceous borders, all framed by their containing walls and hedges.
Tel: 01386 438333
Website: www. nationaltrust.org.uk

The other great garden is virtually next door to Hidcote. Kiftsgate is the creation of three genera-tions of women. The inter-connecting gardens each reveal a distinct character – perhaps reflecting that of their creators. First planted 80 years ago by Heather Muir and devel-oped by her daughter, Kiftsgate is now looked after by Heather's grand-daughter Anne Chambers

and her family. If you are interested in unusual plants in lovely settings, this is the garden for you.
Tel: 01386 438777
Website: www.kiftsgate.co.uk

Blenheim Palace
About 35 miles south of Stratford; take the A3400 through Shipston-on-Stour to Woodstock on the A44
A pleasant three-quarters of an hour drive brings you to one of England's great houses, Blenheim Palace, home to the Duke of Marlborough and the birthplace of Winston Churchill. The palace, in

the pretty village of Woodstock, was built in 1705 for John Churchill, 1st Duke of Marlborough, to commemorate his victory over the French at the Battle of Blenheim. There's a lot to see and do when the palace is open from mid-March to the end of October. The park is open all year round. Entry to the palace includes admission to the permanent Winston Churchill exhibition, the park, butterfly house, train and gardens.
Tel: 01993 811325 (infor-mation line)
Website: www. blenheimpalace.com

WHERE TO STAY

From swish to cosy, ancient manor houses to comfortable family homes, elegant to a touch theatrical, Stratford's accommodation is good and varied. The Tourist Information Centre (see page 94) has a complete list of hotels, guest houses, bed and breakfasts and pubs, as well as self-catering cottages and apartments, and caravan and camping sites.

The list below will give you an idea of the range on offer. Check facilities and prices before booking. The £ symbols are an approximate guide for comparing the prices charged, which range from about £25 to over £100 per person per night.

The Shakespeare Hotel
Chapel Street, Stratford-upon-Avon; map C3
Just as you'd expect in the heart of the town – a lovely picture-postcard, half-timbered building, with 74 bedrooms.
Tel: 0870 400 8182
Website: www.heritage-hotels.com
££££

Ettington Park Hotel
Ettington Park, Alderminster, Stratford-upon-Avon
This magnificent Gothic mansion, 5 miles from the town, is a grand country-house hotel with 48 bedrooms set in grounds that extend to 2,400 hectares (6,000 acres).
Tel: 01789 450123
Website: www.ettingtonpark.co.uk
£££

Hardwick House
1 Avenue Road, Stratford-upon-Avon
Small, family-run, award-winning bed and breakfast guest house with 14 bedrooms, 5 minutes' walk from the town centre.
Tel: 01789 204307
Website: www.stratford-upon-avon.co.uk/hardwick
££

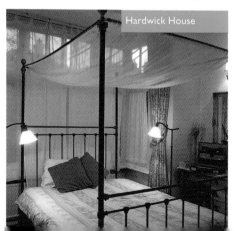

Hardwick House

Melita Hotel
37 Shipston Road,
Stratford-upon-Avon
Comfortable Victorian
house with 12 bedrooms
offering bed and breakfast,
near the town centre.
Tel: 01789 292432
Website: www.
melitahotel.co.uk
££

Victoria Spa Lodge
Bishopton Lane,
Bishopton,
Stratford-upon-Avon
Beautifully furnished, listed
Victorian bed and break-
fast house with seven
bedrooms, a few minutes
drive from the town.
Tel: 01789 267985
Website: www.
stratford-upon-avon.
co.uk/victoriaspa
££

Fox and Goose Inn
Armscote,
Stratford-upon-Avon
If you like the slightly
quirky, you'll love this pub
(see pages 75–76) with its
four stylish bedrooms and
comfortable public rooms.
Armscote is 8 miles south
of Stratford.
Tel: 01608 682293
Website: www.
foxandgoose.co.uk
££

The Crofts Farm
Banbury Road,
Stratford-upon-Avon
Three bedrooms for
guests in this listed
Georgian farmhouse,
5 minutes drive from the
town. Open Apr–Oct.
Garden enthusiasts
especially welcome.
Tel: 01789 292159
Website: www.bbgl.co.uk
££

Folly Farm Cottage
Back Street, Ilmington
Another award-winning
bed and breakfast, with
three bedrooms furnished
in country-cottage style,
7 miles from Stratford.
Tel: 01608 682425
Website:
www.follyfarm.co.uk
££

Graveside
Binton,
Stratford-upon-Avon
Beautiful house set on a
hill in open countryside,
10 minutes' drive from
Stratford. The three bed-
rooms all have wonderful
views – and the breakfast
is good too.
Tel: 01789 750502
Website: www.
stratford-upon-avon.
co.uk/graveside
££

Shakespeare's View
Kings Lane, Snitterfield,
Stratford-upon-Avon
Just two rooms – and
guests have their own
entrance – in this delight-
fully peaceful house,
3 miles north of Stratford.
Tel: 01789 731824
Website:
www.shakespeares.view.
btinternet.co.uk
££

Woodstock Guest House
30 Grove Road,
Stratford-upon-Avon
Comfortable, five-
bedroomed bed and
breakfast, a few minutes'
walk from the centre.
Tel: 01789 299881
Website: www.
stratford-upon-avon.
co.uk/woodstock
£

The Harbour
Salford Road,
Bidford-on-Avon
Three large comfort-
able bedrooms in this
18th-century farmhouse.
There's a swimming pool
too for summer guests.
A 10-minute drive from
Stratford-upon-Avon.
Tel: 01789 772975
Web: www.
theharbour-gh.co.uk
£

U S E F U L
I N F O R M A T I O N

TOURIST INFORMATION

Tourist Information Centre

Bridgefoot, Stratford-upon-Avon CV37 6GW
Extensive range of services, including accommodation booking, travel and events information.
Open: daily; Nov–Mar: Mon–Sat 9.00–17.00; Sun 10.00–16.00; Apr–Oct: Mon–Sat 9.00–18.00; Sun 10.30–16.30
Tel: 01789 293127
Website: www. shakespeare-country. co.uk

Combined tickets

Available from the Tourist Information Centre or from any Shakespeare property. Prices: under £10 for the three houses in Stratford; under £15 for all five Shakespeare properties.

What's on

Look in *Stratford-upon-Avon Herald* on Thursdays, also the bi-monthly 'Focus', free with the *Herald*.

Guided walks

Stratford Town Walk with John and Helen Hogg; tel: 01789 292478 or 07855 760377
Guide Link; tel: 01789 772786
Jo de la Mare; tel: 01926 496077
David Maine; tel: 01527 500865

TRAVEL

By air

Birmingham International Airport is a short drive away. It offers a range of scheduled flights to and from cities in Europe and North America.
Tel: 0121 767 5511

By rail

Stratford railway station is a few minutes' walk from the town centre.

National Rail Enquiry service (daily 24 hours)
Tel: 08457 48 49 50

Virgin Trainline
Tel: 08457 222 333
Central Trains
Tel: 0870 000 6060

Thames Trains (London Paddington to Stratford)
Tel: 08457 300 700

By coach

National Express offers daily services to Stratford.
Tel: 08705 80 80 80

Stagecoach runs a range of services between Stratford, local attractions and other major towns and villages.
Tel: 01788 535555

National Travel Line
Tel: 0870 6082608

Shopmobility

Sheep Street (rear access); map E3
For the loan of manual or powered wheelchairs and electric scooters for those with limited mobility.
Tel: 01789 414534

Taxis

Taxi ranks in Wood Street (map C2), and at the railway station.
Tel: 01789 414007

Car hire
Hertz, Stratford railway
station, off Alcester Road
Tel: 01789 298827

Listers, Western Road
Tel: 01789 294477

Stratford Car and
Commercials, Cophams
Hill Farm; a mile out of
Stratford on the A46
Tel: 01789 295821

Cycle hire
Clarkes Cycles, Guild
Street; map C1
Tel: 01789 205057

PARK AND RIDE
The Park and Ride (signed
from all main routes)
operates on Saturdays
and Bank Holiday Sundays
and Mondays. It's at the
Maybird Centre on the
Birmingham Road. Buses
run every 10 minutes
(15 minutes before 8.30
and after 18.00) to Wood
Street in the town centre.

Car Parks
There are eight car
parks, which are sign-
posted from all
approaches to Stratford.
The Bridgefoot multi-
storey and the adjacent
Unicorn Meadows car
park are both 'Pay on

Foot' – you retain your
ticket and pay on exit.
The others are all pay and
display.
Charges apply 24 hours a
day, seven days a week.

BANKS AND POST OFFICE
Banks and cash dispensers
Barclays, Henley Street;
map C2
Halifax, Bridge Street;
map D2
HSBC, 13 Chapel Street;
map D3
Lloyds TSB, Bridge Street;
map D2
NatWest, Meer Street;
map C2

Main Post Office
2–3 Henley Street;
map C2
Tel: 08457 223344

Bureau de Change
Thomas Cook at HSBC
Bank, 13 Chapel Street;
map D3
Tel: 01789 294688

EMERGENCIES
Fire, ambulance or police
Tel: 999

Stratford Police Station
Rother Street; map B3
Tel: 01789 414111

Hospitals
Stratford-upon-Avon General Hospital
Arden Street; map A1
Casualty (minor injuries)
daily: 7.00–17.00.
Tel: 01789 205831 or
01789 292455

South Warwickshire Hospital
Lakin Road, Warwick
Casualty 24 hours a day,
seven days a week.
Tel: 01926 495321

Emergency vehicle recovery (24 hours)
Arden Garage, Arden
Street; off map B1
Tel: 01789 267446 or (out
of hours) 07836 500155

D. and M. Fancutt
Tel: 01386 830382 or (out
of hours) 07860 835181

24-hour emergency services
Contact Boing UK Ltd for
plumbers, glaziers, etc.
Tel: 0900 587 0548

24-hour petrol station
Shell Station, Shipston
Road (A3400 just south of
Clopton Bridge)

INDEX

CITY-BREAK GUIDES

These full-colour guides come with stunning new photography capturing the special essence of some of Britain's loveliest cities. Each is divided into easy-reference sections where you will find something for everyone – from walk maps to fabulous shopping, from sightseeing highlights to keeping the kids entertained, from recommended restaurants to tours and trips ... and much, much more.

BATH

Stylish and sophisticated – just two adjectives that sum up the delightful Roman city of Bath, which saw a resurgence of popularity in Georgian times and in the 21st century is once again a vibrant and exciting place to be.

CAMBRIDGE

Historic architecture mingles with hi-tech revolution in the university city of Cambridge, where stunning skylines over surrounding fenland meet the style and sophistication of modern city living.

CHESTER

Savour the historic delights of the Roman walls and charming black-and-white architecture, blending seamlessly with the contemporary shopping experience that make Chester such an exhilarating city.

OXFORD

City and university life intertwine in Oxford, with its museums, bookstores and all manner of sophisticated entertainment to entice visitors to its hidden alleyways, splendid quadrangles and skyline of dreaming spires.

STRATFORD

Universally appealing, the picturesque streets of Stratford draw visitors back time and again to explore Shakespeare's birthplace, but also to relish the theatres and stylish riverside town that exists today.

YORK

A warm northern welcome and modern-day world-class shops and restaurants await you in York, along with its ancient city walls, Viking connections and magnificent medieval Minster rising above the rooftops.

Jarrold Publishing, Healey House, Dene Road, Andover, Hampshire, SP10 2AA, UK
Sales: 01264 409206
Enquiries: 01264 409200
Fax: 01264 334110
e-mail: heritagesales@jarrold-publishing.co.uk
website: www.britguides.com

MAIN ROUTES IN AND OUT OF STRATFORD

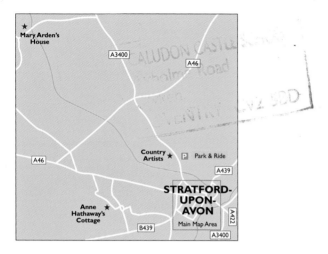

Anne Hathaway's Cottage, Shottery
Signposted from the B439 towards Evesham

Mary Arden's House, Wilmcote
Three miles from Stratford town centre on the A3400

Country Artists Visitors Centre, Avenue Farm
Less than a mile from Stratford town centre on the
A3400 towards Birmingham

**A park and ride service leaves regularly on
Saturdays and bank holiday Sundays and
Mondays for central Stratford from:**

Maybird Centre
On the A3400 towards Birmingham, signposted from
all main routes

See page 95 for further details